CONTAGIOUS FAITH

Discover Your Natural Style for
Sharing Jesus with Others

STUDY GUIDE | SIX LESSONS

MARK MITTELBERG

HarperChristian
Resources

Contagious Faith Training Course Study Guide
© 2021 by Mark Mittelberg

Requests for information should be addressed to:
HarperChristian Resources, 3900 Sparks Dr. SE, Grand Rapids, Michigan 49546

ISBN 978-0-310-12190-9 (softcover)
ISBN 978-0-310-12191-6 (ebook)

HarperChristian Resources titles may be purchased in bulk for church, business, fundraising, or ministry use. For information, please e-mail ResourceSpecialist@ChurchSource.com.

Author is represented by the literary agent Don Gates @ The Gates Group, *www.the-gates-group.com.*

First Printing October 2021 / Printed in the United States of America

CONTENTS

INTRODUCTION

When Jesus gave the Great Commission in Matthew 28:18–20—when he told us to go into all the world to make disciples—he was giving us a mission to share a *contagious faith*. He wanted us to intentionally go into our circles of influence and beyond, telling anyone who would listen about his love and truth. And our goal (borrowing Merriam-Webster's definition of *contagious*) is to *excite similar emotions and conduct in others*—and, I would add, *beliefs* as well.

In so doing, God will use us to infectiously spread our faith to a few other people who will, in turn, carry it to others, who will then relay it to still more. In this way, what Jesus unleashed through his handful of disciples on a hillside two millennia ago will be transmitted through us, and through those we reach, until it ultimately expands to the ends of the earth. In fact, Jesus promised that before he returns, "this gospel of the kingdom will be preached in the whole world as a testimony to all nations" (Matthew 24:14).

It's a lofty vision, but also an exceedingly important and fulfilling one. And it's for all of us who name Christ as our forgiver and leader. More than that, it's a thrilling journey—the most exciting and rewarding thing we can do with our lives.

That said, I understand—you're not so sure about your role in all of this . . . *yet!*

At one time I wasn't sure about my role in it either. But gather with a group and jump into session one. You're in for a wonderful adventure!

How to Use This Guide

The goal of the *Contagious Faith Training Course* is to inspire and equip you and your group to share your faith with others in ways that are natural and fruitful. But the *ultimate* goal is not just to inform our friends about spiritual matters. Rather, it is to help them put their faith in Christ as their leader, forgiver, and king. How will we do this? By helping you discover and deploy your *Contagious Faith Style*, while you learn and grow in a number of *Key Skill* areas that, with the guidance and power of the Holy Spirit will make you increasingly effective at communicating your beliefs to others.

This course is designed to be experienced in a small-group setting, such as a home Bible study or a Sunday school class, as there is a unique dynamic when you learn in the context of relationships. Ultimately, the idea is not just to gain knowledge but also to experience life transformation, to grow in friendships, and to apply what you learn in your day-to-day life. After all, what better way to discover how to share your faith than to be with a group of people who are going through the process with you and learning the same things?

Each participant should have their own copy of this study guide, because you will gain much more from this journey if you are able to write notes in it during the sessions and then to use it to reflect more deeply on the topics covered during the week. It is also helpful to obtain a copy of the *Contagious Faith* book (see the first listing in the "Recommended Resources" section). The videos and material in this study guide are based on information in that book, which develops more fully many of the ideas discussed here.

The *Contagious Faith Training Course* is divided into six sessions— one for each week of the curriculum. Every session contains a Getting Started section to introduce the main topic, some Opening Discussion questions, Video Teaching notes, Group Interaction questions, a Group Activity, Conclusion, and a Closing Challenge.

As a group, you should plan to discuss the opening questions, watch the video, and then use the video notes and questions to engage with the topic. There is complete freedom to decide how best to use these elements to meet the needs of your members. Again, the goal is developing relationships and becoming better equipped to share the gospel with your friends and family members who need to know God—not just "cover the material." You are encouraged to explore each topic as a group and discover what God is saying to you.

These times together as a group can be rewarding, refreshing, and often life-changing. Things might feel a little forced or awkward at first, but don't worry. The members of your group will soon become trusted companions. There is something about learning and praying together that is healthy and invigorating for the soul.

It is important to maintain a positive and safe environment in the group. Members should have an opportunity to share what they are learning to the extent they feel comfortable. Don't feel obligated to participate, but don't keep silent if you have something that contributes to the discussion. People want to hear what you have to say!

On the other hand, no one should dominate the conversation or impose his or her opinions on others. The group discussion time is a conversation, not a monologue or a debate, and differing views are welcome. People are encouraged to share their emotions, challenges, and struggles honestly, without fear of rejection or ridicule. And, of course, it is especially important to maintain confidentiality regarding what is said.

At the end of each group session, there are three optional Between-Sessions Personal Study activities that you are invited to complete on your own. In the first section, Study and Reflect, you will find additional materials that go deeper into the topics previously discussed. The next section, Put It into Practice, will help you develop practical ways to act on the challenge you were given at the end of the group time. In the final section, Reflect on a Key Story, you will find a short reading, usually drawn from the companion book for this course, *Contagious Faith*, by Mark Mittelberg, and a few reflection questions to help you apply its principles to your life.

The goal is simply to engage with these topics on a personal level. You won't be required to divulge what you write, but feel free to bring up questions or things you've learned during the opening discussion at the beginning of the next group meeting. Often, sharing in such a manner is the best way to learn and grow, and you might be surprised at how helpful your thoughts are to others. If you have a busy week and can't get to these activities, don't worry. You are always welcome at the group meetings—ready or not!

Ask for and expect the Holy Spirit to speak to you as you go through this course. It's not an accident that you have chosen to participate in this six-week journey. God has great things in store for you, and he will speak both *to* you and *through* you in ways you might not expect. So take time to pray and listen to what he is saying. You might want to write down some thoughts for future reference. This is the beginning of a deeper walk with Jesus, as well as a new adventure of sharing him with the people in your life.

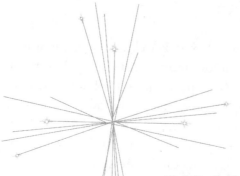

DISCOVERING YOUR CONTAGIOUS FAITH STYLE

There are different kinds of gifts, but the same Spirit distributes them. There are different kinds of service, but the same Lord. There are different kinds of working, but in all of them and in everyone it is the same God at work.

—1 CORINTHIANS 12:4–6

 ## Getting Started

Welcome to session one of the *Contagious Faith Training Course*. I'm glad you decided to join us, and I hope you'll be able to continue with the group throughout these six sessions, as they form building blocks that will expand upon each other. Together, we'll learn how we can naturally and effectively share our faith with the people around us.

Opening Discussion

According to the Bible, we were made not only to know God, but also to introduce him to others. To share the love and truth of Jesus with everyone we can. To reach people for him. To help them find and follow Christ—and then, in turn, to assist them in helping *others* find and follow Christ as well.

"As the Father has sent me," Jesus declared, "I am sending you" (John 20:21). And he added, "You will be my witnesses in Jerusalem, and in all Judea and Samaria, and to the ends of the earth" (Acts 1:8).

Our faith is not just for ourselves. It's not to be hoarded. It's meant to be spread to others. To be infectious. *Contagious.*

If you've been a Jesus-follower for any length of time, you're probably aware of the biblical expectation that we will tell others the Good News about him. But many of us have mixed feelings about that. Let's talk about it.

- What comes to your mind when you hear the word *evangelism*? Positive thoughts? Negative ones? A mix of both?

- This course talks about how our faith can be *contagious.* Obviously, that can be a negative term—but can you think of some things that are contagious in a positive way? What do you think a contagious *faith* might look like?

When we understand it biblically, I believe that developing and sharing a contagious faith is one of the most important and rewarding things we can possibly do. I'll explain this in the video teaching portion of our session, next.

Video Teaching

Now watch the video for session one (see the streaming video access provided on the inside front cover). As you watch, you can use the following outline to record any thoughts or ideas that stand out to you.

Main Teaching

In Matthew 28:18–20, Jesus looked at his disciples—and through them at us—and told them to go into their world and make more disciples. In effect, he was telling all of us who are his followers to develop a *contagious faith*—a faith that will spread to the people around us.

Many of us reflexively respond, "This isn't for me. It's not my gift. It's not my personality. I just want to be an ordinary Christian." I can relate to those feelings of hesitancy. I spent a whole summer in England with my wife Heidi trying to share my faith—mostly in ways that didn't fit me.

Gradually, though, Heidi and I began to innovate. We realized we were more effective when we played to our own strengths, taking roles that best fit each of us, but in partnership with each other.

When we got back home, this approach was reinforced one night at church. Our pastor taught that even in the pages of the New Testament, followers of Jesus shared their faith in a number of ways, or what he described as a variety of evangelism styles. This was liberating to me and encouraged me to keep exploring and developing natural approaches to share my faith.

I spent years adapting and expanding upon these ideas and now teach what I call the five *Contagious Faith Styles*. In the sessions that follow we'll explore each in depth. Here are the five styles:

 Friendship-Building—this employs a relational style that creates a positive environment for spiritual discussions (like Heidi's approach in England)

 Selfless-Serving—this entails helping people in tangible ways that, over time, can open doors to talking about your faith

 Story-Sharing—this approach flows out of your testimony of knowing Jesus, and applies what you've learned to the life of your listener

 Reason-Giving—this involves offering reasons, evidence, and answers that reinforce the trustworthiness of the Christian message (this is Mark's primary style)

 Truth-Telling—this is exhibited by those who are more direct and at times challenging in how they interact with others

During our group interaction time we'll fill out a simple assessment to help each of us discover our primary *Contagious Faith Style*—along with any secondary styles we might have (many of us will have a combination of two or more).

In the sessions that follow we'll also explore and, in some cases, try out some *Key Skills* that will help us become more confident and effective at sharing our faith with others. These skills cut across all the styles and are therefore important for all of us—regardless of what our particular *Contagious Faith Style* happens to be.

Until we've become more comfortable with these *Key Skills*, we'll naturally feel a bit awkward. This is true with any area that's new to us, whether biking, playing tennis or golf, or learning to ski. But what starts out feeling stilted can eventually, through practice, feel natural and even enjoyable. The same is true with developing a contagious faith.

I mentioned that we'll explore some *Essentials for a Contagious Faith* (a few of which I discuss in the video). We'll list all the *Essentials* from the *Contagious Faith* book in our later discussion and give you the chance to reflect more deeply on them, especially in the *Between-Sessions Personal Study* section at the end of this session.

We'll also identify people in our lives who need Christ and pray together for them.

Video Wrap

As a member of the body of Christ, you were called by Jesus to share your faith with others. He wants to use you to communicate his love and truth, and to influence people to follow him. This will become much more natural when you learn and deploy your main *Contagious Faith Style*, and it will become increasingly effective as you understand and hone the *Key Skills* we'll discuss in the sessions to follow.

Contagious Faith Styles Assessment

Now take some time to fill out the *Contagious Faith Styles Assessment*, which will help you identify your primary style as well as any secondary styles you might have. Note that it will probably take you about 6 to 8 minutes to fill out this assessment, including tabulating the results and writing down your top style(s).

Directions

1. Read the 30 statements below, and mark by each of them a number that indicates the degree to which you think that it describes you. Choose from 1 to 5, with 1 being the lowest match, and 5 the highest match.

Here's what each number means:

> 5 That's definitely me.
> 4 That's a lot like me.
> 3 That's somewhat like me.
> 2 That's a little like me.
> 1 That's not me at all.

Don't take a long time thinking about or analyzing the statements. Simply ask "Does this describe me, or not?"— and put down your quick response to each one.

2. As soon as you've marked your response by each of these statements, transfer those numbers to the grid at the end of the questions, and total each column, top to bottom. Then we'll talk about what all of this means. Go ahead and get started—and have fun!

Statements

1. I am a people-person who places a high value on relationships.

2. I recognize needs in people's lives that others often overlook.

3. I often describe my past experiences to illustrate a point I want to make.

4. I'm constantly reading books or articles that help me better understand the issues people are concerned about.

5. When I interact with others I like to get to the point quickly, without a lot of small talk or "beating around the bush."

6. I tend to keep finding more and more new friends.

7. I find fulfillment in helping others, often in behind-the-scenes ways.

8. I often identify with people by making statements like "I used to think the same thing," or "I once experienced something similar to what you've gone through."

9. I tend to be logical, analytical, and inquisitive.

10. I'm generally bold, confident, and direct.

11. I'm usually among the first to extend hospitality to others.

12. I prefer to show love through my actions more than through my words.

13. When I talk about my recent experiences, people seem interested in hearing what I have to say.

14. I'm unsatisfied with merely knowing what I believe, but also want to know *why I believe it*—why it makes sense.

15. I'm fairly comfortable with confronting people with truth, even if it puts a temporary strain on our relationship.

16. I prefer discussing personal matters more than theoretical ideas or current events.

☐ 17. When people seem closed, my quiet demonstration of love and service sometimes makes them more receptive.

☐ 18. I sometimes share my struggles with others in the hope it will help them consider some of the solutions I've found.

☐ 19. I enjoy engaging in discussions and informal debates on challenging questions.

☐ 20. I often take risks to make things better. People generally see me as an agent of change.

☐ 21. I love hanging out with interesting people, sharing a good beverage or meal, and engaging in deeper conversations.

☐ 22. I generally feel more comfortable helping people in a tangible way than getting involved in personal discussions.

☐ 23. People seem interested in hearing stories about things that are happening in my life.

☐ 24. I get frustrated when people use weak arguments or poor logic to try to make a point.

☐ 25. I'm sometimes criticized for coming on too strong in my interactions with others.

☐ 26. People generally consider me attentive, interactive, and responsive.

☐ 27. I tend to be more practical and action-oriented than philosophical and idea-oriented.

☐ 28. I marvel at the ways God reached me, and I'm motivated to tell others about my spiritual journey.

☐ 29. I like to discover and discuss the underlying reasons for the opinions people hold.

☐ 30. I like to get to the bottom of things—to figure out problems and set a course of action, and to make a difference that really matters.

Again, once you have transferred your answers to the appropriate boxes below, add up the numbers in each column, from top to bottom, to discover which of these is your primary *Contagious Faith Style* (based on the highest score), as well as any secondary styles you might have (others that ranked fairly high).

Contagious Faith Styles Assessment Scoring

Friendship- Building	Selfless- Serving	Story- Sharing	Reason- Giving	Truth- Telling
1. ☐	2. ☐	3. ☐	4. ☐	5. ☐
6. ☐	7. ☐	8. ☐	9. ☐	10. ☐
11. ☐	12. ☐	13. ☐	14. ☐	15. ☐
16. ☐	17. ☐	18. ☐	19. ☐	20. ☐
21. ☐	22. ☐	23. ☐	24. ☐	25. ☐
26. ☐	27. ☐	28. ☐	29. ☐	30. ☐

Total ☐ ☐ ☐ ☐ ☐

My primary *Contagious Faith Style*: _____

My secondary *Contagious Faith Style*(s): _____

My secondary *Contagious Faith Style*(s): _____

Group Interaction

Take a few minutes with your group members to discuss what you watched in the video, and then explore the key concepts I presented.

- In the video I described some challenging experiences that Heidi and I went through in trying to reach people for Christ—perhaps similar to some of what your group discussed at the beginning of this session. What was your reaction to what you heard? Did you find the lessons that the two of us learned to be encouraging? Did it give you some fresh ideas for how you might communicate your faith? Take a moment to share thoughts about some of your ideas.

- Now that you have filled out the *Contagious Faith Styles Assessment* and tabulated your totals, would you be willing to share your top style with the group? (Go around the room and let each person reveal what their top style is, along with any secondary styles that ranked fairly high.)

- Are you surprised by the particular *Contagious Faith Style* that came out on top for you? Are any of you *not* surprised by your results—or perhaps by the results of someone else in the group? Why or why not?

- We will learn more about these styles starting in the next session—but based on what you know so far, have you seen your particular style play out in your life somehow (whether in sharing your faith with others, or perhaps in more general ways)? Would you be willing to give an example from your own experience?

 # Group Activity

As I'm sure you're seeing, the central idea for developing a contagious faith is that we can all find a natural approach to sharing Christ with others—our *Contagious Faith Style*. In the sessions that follow we'll unpack each of the five styles, see where they are modeled in the Bible, and discuss steps to develop our particular approaches. We'll also explore a number of *Key Skills* that will help build our confidence in communicating our faith to others.

But right now, let's pick up on something I mentioned briefly in the video: some essential components of a contagious faith. We'll only be able to list and discuss them briefly now, but the *Between-Sessions Personal Study* section will lead you into deeper reflection on these areas. Here are those essentials:

- This Is God's Mission
- This Mission Is for Every Believer
- We Must Have It before We Can Give It Away
- God Can Use Us at Any Stage of Development
- We Must Be Fueled by Love
- We Must Be Grounded in God's Truth
- We Must Communicate through Both Works and Words
- Reaching People Is a Process
- Reaching People Is a Team Activity
- Reaching People Is a Spiritual Activity

Although we haven't had the chance to delve into details yet about these *Essentials for a Contagious Faith*, they are fairly self-explanatory. So let's take a couple minutes to review and consider them.

- Which of these areas strike you as being particularly important? Why?

- Are there any of these that you sense you'll want to focus on as you grow in developing a more contagious faith? Any specific ideas on how you might do so?

 ## Praying for Friends

Before you end your time together, take a few minutes to consider who some of the people are in your life that you'd like to encourage spiritually. They may be family members, longtime friends, neighbors or coworkers, or people you go to school with. It could also be someone you just met but sense that God is up to something in that new acquaintance. In addition, they could be clear-cut non-believers, friends who seem to be on the fence spiritually, or fellow church attenders who might need more clarity related to their relationship with God. You don't need to fully assess their situation to start praying for them or to make yourself available to help them better understand what it means to trust and follow Jesus.

Write down the names of two or three people who come to mind. (Over the course of these sessions, you'll likely think of more friends to pray for. You can come back to this page and add their names here.) Then use this list as a reminder of who you want to lift up to God in prayer.

Now that you've written out a few names, circle the one who you'd like to focus your thoughts on throughout this course, and to pray for right now. This will help you become more intentional in both your prayers for that person and in your interactions with them.

Next, pair up with one other person in your group; briefly tell them who the person is that you'd like to pray for and what you think their general spiritual situation is (be careful not to betray any confidences or to gossip about the person).

Now take several minutes to pray together in pairs, with both of you asking God to open your friends' eyes spiritually, helping them understand his love for them and the truth of his gospel. Pray the Holy Spirit will help them see that they need the forgiveness of the Savior and his leadership in their life. Ask God to guide you on how to "Be wise in the way you act toward outsiders" in order to "make the most of every opportunity" (Colossians 4:5).

Conclusion

We were made to know God and to introduce him to others. And while that might feel a bit challenging right now, it's good to know that we can do this in ways that are congruent with who God made us to be.

He knew what he was doing when he made you. He gave you your natural *Contagious Faith Style(s)*—and now you can stretch within your God-given design to master a few new skills related to sharing your faith. (NOTE: It's okay if you don't neatly fit just one of the styles I've listed. You might be a combination of several of them—or style #6 or #7 that I haven't thought of. I'm not trying to limit your approach but to help you find at least one faith-sharing style that you'll feel comfortable with.) Then as you put these things into practice, you'll be surprised to see how God can use *you* to impact the lives of people around you.

Closing Challenge

As we finish this session, I'd urge you to do a few things: Keep praying for your own growth as you start to develop a contagious faith; also pray for your friends that you'd like to help reach for Christ. Be willing to take a risk and start talking to those friends about spiritual matters, and maybe next week we can hear a couple of stories about what happened!

Finally, I'd urge you to complete the *Between-Sessions Personal Study* and to buy a copy of the *Contagious Faith* book and read the first two chapters (information on the book can be found in the "Recommended Resources" section). Doing so will really enhance your understanding and excitement about the things we're discussing. And then, of course, we'll look forward to seeing you at our next gathering!

Finishing the Session

Briefly close your time in prayer, asking God to use this training course to equip and inspire every member to make the most of what you're learning, and to use each of you to have an eternal influence on the lives of those you each hope to reach.

BETWEEN-SESSIONS PERSONAL STUDY

You can grow in the areas we covered during the first session of the *Contagious Faith Training Course* by engaging in the following between-sessions activities. The time you invest here will help deepen your understanding of, and excitement for, what we're learning together.

📖 Section One: Study and Reflect

Take some time before our next gathering to reflect on the evangelism essentials that we looked at briefly during our first session. These are listed below with a brief explanation of each (you can read more details on all of them in chapter one of the *Contagious Faith* book). As you do, ask God to show you areas that you should concentrate on in order to grow more prepared and more effective at sharing your faith with others. Also, write down any specific thoughts or next steps you want to take in the space under each of these essentials.

Essentials for a Contagious Faith

1. This Is God's Mission.
Reaching people with the gospel was not *our* idea. It's not something we came up with and are now asking God to help us accomplish. No, it's the opposite. It was the heavenly Father who "so loved the world

that he gave his one and only Son, that whoever believes in him shall not perish but have eternal life" (John 3:16)—and now he invites us into *his* mission of reaching others.

2. This Mission Is for Every Believer.

Jesus said, "Go and make disciples of all nations, baptizing them in the name of the Father and of the Son and of the Holy Spirit, and teaching them to obey everything I have commanded you" (Matthew 28:19–20). These words are for *everyone* who is a genuine follower of Jesus. This is not a mission that's reserved for people with certain gifts, talents, or callings. It's a task that we all need to do our part to complete together.

3. We Must Have It before We Can Give It Away.

Evangelism has been described as *overflow*—it's letting what we have in Christ spill over into the lives of those around us. But that means we need to genuinely know and walk with him first. Are there things you need to get right with him? Don't gloss over this question, even if you've been part of a church for a long time. David wrote, "Search me, God, and know my heart; test me and know my anxious thoughts. See if there is any offensive way in me, and lead me in the way everlasting" (Psalm 139:23–24). I'd urge you to pray the same prayer, and to respond to anything God shows you. As honestly and completely as you know how, receive his forgiveness and leadership—and then let him guide you into this great adventure of reaching others.

4. God Can Use Us at Any Stage of Development.

Most of us get caught up thinking we're too young, or too old, or too inexperienced, or too undereducated to really be used by God in the lives of others. But that's a lie. As has often been said, God is not looking for *ability* as much as he's looking for *availability*. If you'll let him, he can work through you. As Paul encouraged his young apprentice, Timothy, "Be prepared in season and out of season . . . do the work of an evangelist," (2 Timothy 4:2, 5). Here's the truth: most of us feel "out of season" most of the time. But if we'll make ourselves available to him, he knows how to make up the difference, using us at whatever current stage of development we might happen to be.

5. We Must Be Fueled by Love.

If you're driven to share your faith by any motivation other than love, then you're running on the wrong fuel. Our mission is ultimately not to win arguments, to prove people wrong, to get them to do what we want them to do, or to join our church or cause. No, it's to lovingly point them to the Savior so that they, too, can experience the love and forgiveness of our gracious God. Are you sensing God's love in your life these days? Does it encourage you to share his love with others? If not, then make this a matter of prayer, asking him to expand your heart for him and for the people in your life.

6. We Must Be Grounded in God's Truth.

It might seem self-evident that we need to be rooted in the teachings of the Bible, but unfortunately that's no longer obvious to some people. More and more self-proclaimed Christians are talking about God and telling people what they think he wants for their lives, but they do so without stopping to consult his actual revelation to make sure they're telling people the right things about him. If you want to lead others into the faith, then you must first make certain that the faith you're leading them into is anchored in the clear and consistent doctrines of God's Holy Word, the Bible.

7. We Must Communicate through Both Works *and* Words.

Many believers think if they just live an authentic Christian life, then others will see it and be drawn to it. But that is, at best, a half-truth. It's correct that our actions really matter, and they can be highly attractive to the people we hope to reach. But Paul asked in Romans 10:14 (NLT): "How can they call on him to save them unless they believe in him? And how can they believe in him if they have never heard about him? And how can they hear about him unless someone tells them?" I paraphrase Paul's point like this: "Your friends are never going to *see it*, unless you go to them and *say it*." Good works can open hearts; grace-filled words can open minds. The Holy Spirit can use the two elements together to redeem lives for eternity.

8. Reaching People Is a Process.

Those we hope to reach rarely move from spiritual doubt or disinterest all the way over to trust in Christ in one fell swoop. Instead, the journey usually takes time. Therefore, we need to be willing to walk with friends over the long haul as they consider Christianity. Remember that Jesus himself taught that those considering following him should first count the cost of becoming his disciple (Luke 14:25–35). In effect, he was urging them to slow down and make sure they knew what they were committing to before signing on. We need to anticipate, therefore, that this will often be a longer, step-by-step process. Then we should do all we can to try to facilitate that process by helping our friends stay on the path as they move toward Christ.

9. Reaching People Is a Team Activity.

It's intimidating to think that the process of someone coming to faith in Jesus is all dependent on you. Fortunately, that's almost *never* the case. Paul illustrated this in 1 Corinthians 3:5–6: "What, after all, is Apollos? And what is Paul? Only servants, through whom you came to believe—as the Lord has assigned to each his task. I planted the seed, Apollos watered it, but God has been making it grow." See how the process works? We are simply instruments in God's skillful hands, contributing our own small voice to the symphony he's orchestrating. We can each play a unique role (or several roles) in the divine effort God is directing to bring people into his family.

10. Reaching People Is a Spiritual Activity.

Helping people come to Christ is not just a matter of giving them good information or answers to their questions and objections. Neither is it just about being passionate or persuasive—though all of these can be important. It is, at bottom, a *spiritual* struggle that is being fought at an unseen level, and because of this we are *all* out of our league and need God's wisdom, help, and intervention. Ultimately, it is the Holy Spirit who draws people into God's loving arms. Therefore, we need to be as attuned to him and his workings as possible. This will come only through spending deep and consistent times with him in prayer, as well as regularly studying God's Word, the Bible. "If you remain in me and I in you," Jesus promised in John 15:5, "you will bear much fruit." And don't miss his next phrase: ". . . apart from me you can do nothing."

Section Two: Put It into Practice

• Which of these *Essentials for a Contagious Faith* stood out as areas you need to better understand or work on?

• Are there specific next steps you sense you need to take? What will you do, and when?

• The last of these essentials reminds us that this is a *spiritual* activity. That's why we prayed with another group member for someone in each of your lives, asking God to open their eyes and to draw them spiritually. Take some time to pray for those names again now, and perhaps for others on the list you began.

• Is there anyone else who you sense you should add to that list and start praying for?

Also, take a moment to pray for yourself—asking God to strengthen you in the areas we're discussing during this study and to give you wisdom concerning any other next steps you should take.

Section Three: Reflect on a Key Story

The following is a story from the companion book for this course, *Contagious Faith*. Read it and then respond to a few reflection questions afterward.

GOD USES ORDINARY CHRISTIANS—LIKE US!

Why me? I wondered.

Why would God ask someone like me—who just weeks earlier had been recklessly partying and resisting him—to be the one to talk about spiritual stuff to someone like Peggy?

It wasn't that I didn't want to encourage her. We had been friends in high school, we were on the drama team and in a few of the same plays, and we'd even been at some parties together. But now my life had changed radically. I'd trusted in Christ, though I wasn't quite sure what that was going to look like.

Peggy had recently started visiting a Bible study that I attended, and I'd been sensing that God wanted me to talk to her about it. I couldn't get away from the concern that she was becoming acclimated to our Christian culture but missing the central point of what it means to become a true follower of Christ.

But, again, why me? I barely knew what I was doing. I was only nineteen years old and had put my trust in him less than two months earlier. I had not been trained to share my faith. I hadn't been through any evangelism courses. I felt like a novice when it came to discussing God's activity in my life . . . because, well, I *was* a novice. I just knew that I needed to do so, and I was willing to try—even if it meant feeling awkward in the process. As I was crossing the Eighth Street Bridge in our hometown, I saw Peggy walking alone on the snow-packed sidewalk.

I was surprised that anyone would be out for a stroll on such a frigid December day, but I believed this could be the opportunity God had been pointing me toward.

I pulled my car to the side of the road and rolled down the passenger window to say hello (yes, we actually had to *roll down* our windows in those days). We chatted for a few minutes, and then I mentioned the study group. She told me she was enjoying it, loved meeting so many new friends, and was learning from the discussions.

"I'm glad you're growing in your understanding of God and the Bible," I said, as I took a deep breath and tried to sound more confident than I actually felt. "But there's something I've been meaning to ask you."

"What's that?" Peggy replied.

"I'm curious to know . . ." I said, trying to muster the courage to get to the heart of the matter, ". . . whether you've ever really asked for Jesus's forgiveness and committed your life to him?" "No, I've never done that," Peggy said. "And nobody has ever told me I needed to!"

I'm not sure what I was so afraid of. Maybe I was worried that Peggy would think I was judging her, or that I was trying to push her into a commitment she wasn't ready to make. Or perhaps it was the very real possibility that she would be open and ready to trust in Christ—but I wouldn't say things clearly and instead would squander the opportunity. Whatever the source of my trepidation, it turned out to be an unwarranted concern.

"Well," I replied, feeling a tinge of Holy Spirit-inspired confidence, "you really *do* need to ask Jesus for his forgiveness and leadership in your life." Then I started doing my best to explain what that means, including telling her how I had given my life to Christ just weeks earlier.

To my relief, she seemed receptive—but she also let me know she needed to get back home soon for a family dinner. She quickly added that she'd like to continue talking later that evening, if I'd be willing to swing by. I said I would, and I silently prayed that God would move in her heart, opening her to the gospel.

When we picked up the discussion later that night, I found out that God had been working in Peggy's life in a variety of ways. She had a formal church background but had walked away from it in junior high. Now, after graduating from high school and spending a summer working at Yellowstone National Park, Peggy had a renewed interest in spiritual matters. In fact, God was speaking to her through a Bible she had "stolen" from a hotel room in Yellowstone (not realizing that the Gideons put them there *hoping* people will "steal" them); through several of her Christian friends; through our Bible study; through a service at a church the night before; and now through our interactions.

By the time our conversation was over, Peggy was ready to ask Jesus for his forgiveness and guidance in her life. With my heart beating fast, I did my fledgling best to lead her in a coherent prayer of repentance and faith. In spite of my inadequacies, the Holy Spirit worked in a powerful way—and Peggy's life and eternity were changed. What a thrill it was for me to help seal her relationship with God!

And how exhilarating it will be for *you* to be used in similar ways—whether you feel up to the task yet or not!

As I mentioned at the end of the session, between now and when your group meets again, I recommend reading chapters 1 and 2 of the *Contagious Faith* book, where you'll get more encouragement and hear additional stories of how God wants to use ordinary believers like us. You'll also find out the rest of the story about the amazing ways God worked in and through Peggy's life in the years following her initial commitment to Christ!

(?) Reflection Questions

1. Have you ever sensed, like I did with Peggy, that there was someone God was prompting you to talk to about him? What did you do?

2. Is there someone you feel God wants you to talk to now—or at least get closer—to so that you'll be able to talk to that person soon? What next step could you take now to start moving in that direction?

3. I was a new believer when I had that conversation with Peggy, yet God worked in spite of my inexperience. Have you been letting your own inexperience, or maybe lack of biblical knowledge, or something similar keep, you from being available to God? If so, pray about that now and ask God to help you overcome whatever has been limiting you.

4. In Matthew 28, right after Jesus told his disciples—and us—to go into our world to share the Good News and make more disciples, he added this: "And surely I am with you always, to the very end of the age" (verse 20). How does this promise from Jesus encourage you to take more risks to reach out to people in your circle?

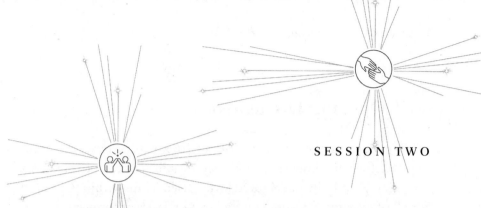

INITIATING RELATIONSHIPS AND SERVING OTHERS

Be wise in the way you act toward outsiders; make the most of every opportunity. Let your conversation be always full of grace, seasoned with salt, so that you may know how to answer everyone.

— COLOSSIANS 4:5–6

 ## Getting Started

Welcome back to session two of our study! Today we're talking about how we can build friendships with unbelievers and serve them in ways that can draw them to Christ. We'll also explore the first two of the five *Contagious Faith Styles* that are related to these areas—*Friendship-Building* and *Selfless-Serving*.

In the first session you filled out the assessment to determine your primary style, along with any secondary ones. Did you get the chance to try one of those styles since that meeting? How did it go? Also, did you have any opportunities or breakthroughs with any of the friends you were praying for?

It's interesting how often God starts opening doors to spiritual interactions once we start preparing ourselves and praying for the people around us!

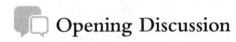 Opening Discussion

While people may seem closed spiritually, they're usually open relationally. Whether they know it or not, they are still created in the image of a relational God who has enjoyed loving friendships within the Trinity for all of eternity. No wonder we all crave relational connections and, no surprise, we hurt so badly when those are torn apart. Our need for deep personal connectedness is woven into the very fabric of what it means to be human.

People need people, and friends listen to friends. Just think of who *you* turn to when you're going through a hard time or need someone to speak into your life. Probably not some religious person who shows up at your door or sends you an unsolicited email. No, we naturally want to talk to someone who we know and trust and who we are confident will have our best interests at heart. In other words, we want to turn to a real friend.

That's probably why survey after survey shows that a high percentage of Christians came to Christ primarily through the influence of a close friend or family member.

• Would you say that you came to faith mostly through the efforts of someone you knew? If so, who was that person?

• As you saw in the last session, reaching people is usually a process that happens over time, and it almost always includes multiple conversations. Was that true with the person God used to reach you?

Likewise, when we selflessly meet the needs of others, we demonstrate to them that they are valuable and loved—both by God and by us, his children—regardless of the barriers they've erected. In effect, we get behind the wall with them and, over time, help them tear it down, brick by brick. It may take a while, but the ways we serve them can help them become more open spiritually, eventually leading them to trust in Jesus. As he put it in the Sermon on the Mount, "Let your light shine before others, that they may see your good deeds and glorify your Father in heaven" (Matthew 5:16).

- Would you say that you came to faith at least in part because someone showed you that kind of selfless service? If so, what did the person do for you?

 # Video Teaching

Now let's watch the teaching video for this session (once again, you can find the streaming video access information provided on the inside front cover). As you watch, use this outline to record any ideas you want to be sure and remember.

Main Teaching

Years after the experience of sharing our faith in London, Heidi and I moved to a small town where we soon had the chance to meet our neighbors and, once again, saw God use Heidi's *Friendship-Building* style. We hit it off with a woman named Kathy, along with her fiancé, Don. Heidi and Kathy started interacting about spiritual matters, and occasionally I'd get involved in addressing questions of faith.

The friendship between Heidi and Kathy grew over the months, and things came to a head when Kathy visited our home one morning. Her questions led not only to us sharing some biblical answers but also to presenting the gospel—and Kathy ended up praying with us to receive Christ.

Kathy's life changed dramatically, and soon she was sharing her new-found faith with the people around her. And, like Heidi, Kathy's main approach is now the *Friendship-Building* style.

Our biblical example of the *Friendship-Building Contagious Faith Style* is Matthew, the tax collector-turned-follower of Christ. Luke 5:29 tells us he had a banquet at his house and invited his former coworkers along with Jesus and the other disciples. Matthew's party formed a great environment for spiritual conversations.

Jesus, too, often used the *Friendship-Building* approach. In fact, in the gospel Matthew would later write, he reported that Jesus was sometimes called "the friend of sinners" (Matthew 11:19).

Those with the *Friendship-Building* style are people-people. They're all about relationships, and they tend to focus in on the other person's life and situation. And God often works through these kinds of friendships to draw people to himself.

There are some important *Key Skills* related to initiating and strengthening friendships as well as starting spiritual conversations that all of us need to learn. (Here's an abbreviated outline, and we'll focus on them more during our group discussion time):

1. **Start and Strengthen Relationships**
2. **Initiate Spiritual Conversations**
3. **Invite Friends into Life-Changing Environments**

The other approach we're unpacking in this session is the *Selfless-Serving* style. We see this one modeled in the story of a woman named Grace and her mother, who served a man named Morris when his house was flooding during a hurricane. This loving service started a chain of events that ultimately led him to put his trust in Jesus.

Our biblical example of *Selfless-Serving* is Tabitha (also known as Dorcas), in Acts 9. She made articles of clothing for those who were in need. She was like a first-century Mother Teresa, serving in ways that made people look heavenward and realize there must be a God.

Jesus, of course, modeled the *Selfless-Serving* style as well. He fed people, and he taught and encouraged them. He sometimes healed them or their family members. And, ultimately, he served all of us by selflessly laying down his life to pay for our sins and pave the way for our salvation.

Those with the *Selfless-Serving* approach recognize people's needs and find joy in helping meet those needs. They serve others in tangible ways, and this loving service can often open those folks up to the God who motivates their serving. In fact, those of you with this approach will often end up reaching the hardest-to-reach people.

Once again, there are some *Key Skills* that we all need to learn related to serving others in ways that will not only bless them but that can also open them up to hearing about the God we represent. (Here's a brief list of those skills; we'll explore them more in our between-sessions section of this study guide):

1. **Nurture a Spirit of Empathy**
2. **Make Room for Divine Interruptions**
3. **Develop Discernment about Who to Serve**

Interview

Now let's meet author and pastor Rashawn Copeland and his wife, Denisse. Rashawn wrote a powerful book called *Start Where You Are* (see the "Recommended Resources" section in the back of this study guide for details on Rashawn's book and his and Denisse's ministry). One of Rashawn's primary approaches is the *Friendship-Building* style, while Denisse mostly uses the *Selfless-Serving* approach.

Video Wrap

I hope you were encouraged by Rashawn and Denisse's examples of building friendships and sacrificially serving those outside the family, as well as by their infectious personalities! They really do exemplify what a contagious faith can look like—and they are inspiring models of how God can use the *Friendship-Building* and *Selfless-Serving* approaches.

 # Group Interaction

In light of the teaching you just heard, let's talk about these first two areas. (NOTE: Because we're covering two styles in this session, you'll need to keep these interactions fairly brief.)

- Based on the discussions in the video, as well as the assessment that you filled out last week, do you think the *Friendship-Building* style is likely your main approach? Or might it be a secondary style for you?

- Or would you say that the *Selfless-Serving* style is your primary approach? One of your secondary styles?

- If you raised your hand for either of those first two styles, would you be willing to share a next step you think you'll take to try out that approach? Or maybe give a brief example of something you've already done that fits your style? And what about the rest of us—any quick thoughts on how you might grow in these areas as well?

Now let's interact on some of the *Key Skills* I mentioned in the video. These will be broadly related to the first style we discussed, *Friendship-Building* (we'll cover the remaining *Key Skills* related to the *Selfless-Serving* style in our between-sessions materials). Whether or not the *Friendship-Building* style is your primary approach, here are the first two *Key Skills* all of us should put into practice.

Key Skill #1: Start and Strengthen Relationships
Relationships form the best foundation for almost every kind of personal evangelism. But where should we begin? As I explained in the video, there are several areas:

- *Deepen Current Friendships.* Usually what we need with the people we already know is to go deeper with them. It's easy to get stuck at a superficial level with friends and family. Can you describe an idea of something you could do to initiate closer relationships with people you already know?

- *Renew Lapsed Friendships.* We all have people in our lives we used to know, and who we thought we'd stay close to—but over time we've grown apart. Who are some friends from your past that are coming to mind? Can you mention who you might look up in order to reestablish the relationship?

- *Start New Friendships.* There may be people around you that you don't know, but who the Holy Spirit is nudging you to reach out to. It may be a new classmate, a fresh recruit at work, or someone who just moved into the neighborhood. Can you share an example of a person who God might be bringing to your attention?

As you think about these areas of relationships, more people may be coming to mind to pray for. If so, go back to the page in session one where we started writing down names, and add any new ones. And then pray for them this week, asking God to help open up opportunities to interact with them.

Key Skill #2: Initiate Spiritual Conversations

We've looked at ways to establish and deepen relationships, but in order to have a spiritual influence we'll need to initiate spiritual conversations. We must put our beliefs into words. Here are three approaches I mentioned in the video. (You or someone in the group can read the following three options, and then we'll try one of them.)

- *Bridge from Standard Topics to Spiritual Ones.* For example, your friend is talking about a sports team, so you mention a player you know to be a Christian. Or you're discussing music, so you mention a song that raises spiritual issues.

- **Ask Curiosity Questions.** You can ask something like, "I'm curious, do you ever think about spiritual matters?" Or, "What is your religious background? Is it something you still practice now?"

- **Turn Invitations into Conversations.** Many people will come with us to a church service or Christian event if we'll invite them. But even when they won't, some will still be willing to talk about it. You can say, "I'm sorry you can't go . . . Have you ever been to something like this?" You'll be off to a great conversation!

Now let's give this a try.

 # Group Activity

Practice Starting a Spiritual Conversation

Our goal is to *train* all of us to put these ideas into practice—but *training always involves trying.* So let's try the *Key Skill* we just discussed—getting into a significant conversation by bridging from an ordinary topic to a spiritual one.

Scan the three scenarios below, choose the one you want to use, and write down an idea or two of things you could say to bridge from that topic to a spiritual one. Then pair up with someone in the group, tell them which scenario you're going to try, and roleplay a conversation with them about that topic, turning it toward spiritual matters. Then after you've practiced, reverse roles and have the other person roleplay using the scenario that they chose.

Yes, roleplaying like this might feel a bit artificial. But simple practice times like this will help you feel more comfortable in initiating a real conversation with someone you hope to encourage spiritually. (Note: This practice will probably take about 5–6 minutes total. Have fun!)

❑ *Beautiful sunset.* You're outside talking to a friend or neighbor, and gradually the sky starts getting more and more colorful—to the point where you both comment on it. What could you say to bridge from that gorgeous sunset to the topic of the Creator?

❑ *Personal suffering or disappointment.* You're talking to a friend about a recent loss in their life (the death of a relative, a bad medical report, losing a job, or similar). How might you gently bridge from that difficult situation to the comfort or help available through Christ?

❑ *Upcoming holiday.* You're bantering with someone at school or work about the rapidly approaching Christmas or Easter holiday, and what they're planning to do that day. How might you bridge from discussing typical activities to deeper spiritual meaning?

How did it go? Were you able to bridge the conversation in a way that felt fairly natural to you? What did you say to open a spiritual topic of conversation?

Would you say something different if you could try it again? (Probably so—that's why practice times are so important. You likely did pretty well, but you're already thinking of ways you might do it better. That's why we need to keep practicing, both here and out there with the friends and family members we'd like to reach!)

 # Conclusion

This has been a very full session (it's the only one in which we'll explore two *Contagious Faith Styles* in succession), so thanks for hanging in there with me. We learned about both the *Friendship-Building* and the *Selfless-Serving* styles, and we met a great couple who uses these two approaches in partnership with each other. I hope you feel encouraged not only by their inspiring examples, but also by the potential we all have to partner with each other in synergistic ways—though I'm getting ahead of myself. That's a topic we'll discuss in a later session!

 # Closing Challenge

I want to end this session with this. Don't just *think about* building friendships with people you'd like to share your faith with—and don't just *practice* getting into spiritual conversations. And don't simply *imagine* serving people in ways that might open them up to the Lord. Instead, *put these things into practice this week!* Prayerfully look for opportunities, and when you see them, be sure to seize them!

Does that make you a little nervous? That's natural. You're learning something new, but remember that we're all here to pray for and support each other. And you know what else? You won't be out there alone. No, as we've mentioned, Jesus promised that as you go into your world to share his Good News, he will be with you—literally—through the person of the Holy Spirit.

So go. Take a few small risks this week. See how God uses your efforts. And then come back to our next section with some great stories to tell!

And be sure and engage with the *Between-Sessions Personal Study* materials at the end of this section of the study guide before we meet again. Especially focus on the important *Key Skills* related to serving others in selfless ways—ways that will help draw them to the Savior.

Also, let me urge you to read chapters 3 and 4 of the *Contagious Faith* book, where you'll hear more stories and get more inspiration related to the things we've covered.

 ## Finishing the Session

Before closing, pray together. Bring to your mind that main person you're focusing on during this course. Lift that person up to the Lord, asking God to open their eyes, to work in their heart, and to draw them to Christ. Also ask him to give you greater boldness and confidence so you'll be willing to take risks for the sake of the gospel and for the salvation of these people who you love.

BETWEEN-SESSIONS PERSONAL STUDY

During the discussion time in our last session, we focused on *Key Skills* related to the areas of building relationships and initiating spiritual conversations. Those areas are fundamental practices regardless of our specific *Contagious Faith Styles*—and they are the main tools for those with the *Friendship-Building* approach.

What we'll do now in this between-sessions section is hit one more *Key Skill* related to relationships (#3: how to effectively invite friends to church services or other Christian events), as well as cover three *Key Skills* related to serving people in ways that can also open them up to our message. These form a foundation of compassion that will help us extend God's love and truth to people in virtually any situation.

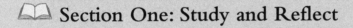 Section One: Study and Reflect

The Remaining Key Skill Related to Building Friendships

Key Skill #3: Invite Friends into Life-Changing Environments.
(This was the third of the *Key Skills* related to friendship-building that I discussed in the last video.)

Don't underestimate the potential of bringing friends to a church service or spiritual discussion group. It's not just a matter of the information they'll hear, but also the experience of sitting among believers who are singing heartfelt songs of worship. It's watching us pray to our living Savior. It's feeling the presence of God's Spirit and sensing that he is touching their hearts and awakening them to their need for salvation. So how can we effectively invite people? Here are three thoughts:

- *Tailor Invitations to Interests and Needs.* Invite your friends to events that will address their particular questions, meet needs they're concerned about, or just be something you think they'd enjoy. This might be as simple as asking neighbors to come to church when your pastor will be speaking on a topic that is relevant to them—such as what the Bible says about how to have a better marriage or build a stronger family. Your invitation will be attractive if you tailor it to their interests, questions, or concerns.

- *Provide Printed Information.* You'll greatly increase the odds of getting your friend to attend if you put something printed in his or her hands. It should include all the information they need regarding when and where the event is, how to park, where to register, and so forth. Eliminating confusion about the details will go a long way toward easing their concerns and helping them say yes.

- *Bring Your Friend with You.* By far the best way to get your friends to show up is to bring them with you. So, after explaining what the event is and why you think they'd enjoy it, and after giving them printed information, offer to pick them up and go together. Better yet, if there's a cost for the event tell them you'll buy their ticket and even take them out for coffee or a meal afterward. This will make the invitation attractive—and who knows how God might use it to work in their life?

Do these ideas bring some friends to mind? What can you do this week to encourage a friend or family member to attend a church service, Christian event, or small group discussion with you?

Key Skills Related to Serving Others

1. Nurture a Spirit of Empathy.

We must nurture the attribute of empathy in order to foster the right spirit behind serving others.

This value, unfortunately, is lacking in many people's lives. And without it, we end up preoccupying ourselves mostly with our own needs, easily overlooking the concerns of the people around us. This is only encouraged by the spirit of our age, in which people are increasingly "lovers of themselves, lovers of money" (2 Timothy 3:2). These days, looking out for the needs of others is truly countercultural.

So how can we grow in this area? In part, by asking ourselves the classic question "What would Jesus do?" whenever we see someone in need of help or encouragement. The more we see people through his eyes, and then serve them with his spirit of empathy and concern, the more we'll be able to open them up to his love and truth.

2. Make Room for Divine Interruptions.

In order to be effective in reaching others for Christ, we need to manage our schedules, as well as our attitudes, in light of *divine interruptions*. Have you ever noticed that much of Jesus's ministry happened in the midst of interruptions? As he was "leaving the city" (Mark 10:46), for instance, a blind man called out to him. It would have been easy for Jesus to say to his disciples, "Sorry, guys, it's not on the agenda. We have other obligations to fill, so tell him it'll have to wait."

Can you imagine? Instead, Jesus asked the man what he wanted, and he ended up restoring the man's sight. All on his way out of town!

We need to learn to manage our lives so we can be open and watching for the divine interruptions God might bring our way this week, as he attracts people to us who need to be served in the name of Christ. These situations might feel challenging—scratch that, they *will* feel challenging—but the impact of your response can be both exponential and eternal.

3. Develop Discernment about Who to Serve.

There's one more essential skill we need to address: Knowing when to serve and when not to. Why is this so important? Because there will be an endless array of needs around you, and you'll never be able to meet them all—though you could die trying!

It's fascinating to see that the same Savior who was so open to divine interruptions was also willing to walk away (or sometimes *sail* away) from situations where there were still more people who needed to be healed, fed, or encouraged. If even the incarnate Son of God had to pass on certain situations, then you and I will certainly need to do so as well.

That's why we need the wisdom of Scripture and the guidance of the Holy Spirit. God is able to lead us to say no to many opportunities so that we can say yes to the right ones, and then back up our yeses with wholehearted love and action. Learning this skill, and discerning God's direction concerning who, where, and how long to serve, will enable us to help others in more strategic ways and therefore have a greater impact over the long haul.

Are there areas related to these *Key Skills* that you need to focus on? What do you sense God telling you to do?

Is there someone in your world who you know needs some kind of help that you could offer? What will you commit to doing? Step out and see how God can use such others-centered actions to open them up to his love and truth.

 ## Section Two: Put It into Practice

As you seek to build more redemptive relationships with people outside of God's family, and as you serve them in selfless ways, pay heed to the following cautions related to these two areas.

Cautions Related to Friendship-Building

- *Stay Genuine.* First, make sure your relational efforts are genuine, and that you present yourself and your intentions honestly. No one wants to be manipulated. Don't feign a friendship in order to try to move someone toward Christ. That will backfire, and it won't properly represent our Savior, who was always forthright with others. Rather, extend yourself as a real friend as it seems appropriate—but make sure you aren't attaching any strings or conditions to the relationship. Show genuine love for the person whether they agree with you or not. And don't hide the fact that part of how you love people is by telling them the truth about God and his gracious offer of forgiveness and salvation. You want to be a real friend *and* you want to introduce them to the greatest Friend they could ever know.

- *Establish Boundaries.* Avoid misunderstandings with members of the opposite gender. Some say that in our promiscuous times it's too risky to try sharing Jesus with the other sex. I understand that concern, but I disagree with the conclusion. Remember that Jesus reached out to the Samaritan woman in John 4—commonly known as "the woman at the well." But he was wise in how he did this, talking to her in broad daylight and in a public place. The result? Not only did he lead this precious woman to trust in him, but through her, many of her friends were also reached, and it helped form the first fellowship of Jesus followers in her little town in Samaria.

- *Prioritize Truth.* Here's one more important caution related to building relationships with those outside the family: Beware of valuing friendship over truth. In other words, don't get so caught up in having a smooth relationship that you shrink back from sharing the gospel with your friend. Telling the person that they are a sinner who needs a Savior can create ripples in the relational pond—but if we really love them, then we must be willing to take that risk. That's what real friendship demands: caring about the other person enough to tell them what they need to hear. If they are headed for disaster—especially in the spiritual realm—you might have to tell them some unpleasant truths in order to protect them from what's coming. The Bible reflects the same concern. According to Proverbs 27:5–6, "Better is open rebuke than hidden love. Wounds from a friend can be trusted, but an enemy multiplies kisses."

Cautions Related to Serving Selflessly

- **Serve without Conditions.** Make sure that when you serve others you don't do so in a conditional way. Our service needs to be motivated by love and care, with no strings attached. As soon as we start proportioning our willingness to help based on the other person's level of spiritual openness, they will feel they're being manipulated—and rightly so. If you read John 13 carefully, you'll notice that Jesus washed the feet of *all* of his disciples, including Judas, who he knew would betray him later that very night. Christ's service was not conditioned on how they were responding to his love and friendship. We need to follow his example.

- **Explain What Motivates You.** Beware of the dangerous tendency to serve silently. People who serve others are often less vocal, preferring to show their love in quiet but tangible ways. That's okay, but at some point it's important to let the person know that it's the love of Christ that motivates you. You can do this in ways that fit you, whether with a simple word, a written note, the gift of a Christian book, or maybe an invitation to your church or another Christian event. Just don't leave them thinking you're simply genetically predisposed to being nice. As Jesus said in Matthew 5:16, "Let your light shine before others, *that they may see your good deeds and glorify your Father in heaven*" (emphasis mine). But how will they know to glorify the Father unless we somehow direct their attention to him?

- *Practice Patience.* One more caution is in order. You're going to need patience. Sacrificially serving others can reach the hardest-to-reach people—but that rarely happens quickly. Some of the barriers people have constructed to keep out God are well established and strong. There are people who have been so deeply hurt by the church or by religious people that they're going to be extra cautious. Helping someone in that situation take down their wall "brick by brick" can be a long and sometimes arduous process. Don't expect rapid results, and resist getting frustrated. Just keep serving selflessly and consistently pray for the people you serve, knowing that God is working in and through you. He knows how, over time, to help them *"see your good deeds and glorify your Father in heaven."*

 ## Section Three: Reflect on a Key Story

The following stories are drawn the *Contagious Faith* book. Read through them and consider the reflection steps at the end of these accounts.

 # THE POTENTIAL IN BUILDING FRIENDSHIPS

Julie was one of the shyest people I had ever met. Back in my early days of ministry in Chicago, she was so quiet and reserved that she would almost whisper when she talked to me. Yes, she was friendly—and she really did like people. But I'm pretty sure if you would have looked up the word *introvert* in the dictionary, you'd find a picture of Julie.

The good news, though, is that she was motivated to share the Good News with others. She would often meet with me to ask for ideas on how to reach out to her family members. She would read any articles or books I would recommend. She would look up things I'd suggest she research. And when I urged her to come to our evangelism seminar, she showed up for the class. In fact, Julie ended up taking those early renditions of our training course multiple times.

Gradually, Julie's confidence in talking about her faith began to grow. In her own reserved and quiet way, Julie built and deepened relationships with the people she hoped to spiritually influence. It wasn't long before she led her husband to Christ. Then her parents. Then her teenage daughters. Then a few nephews, and some of their friends. She even led a visitor at our church to trust in Jesus during a tour of the building. In fact, in one year's time, Julie led *fourteen people* to faith in Christ.

And you know what? Julie is *still* shy and introverted. She's exactly who God made her to be—and he delights to work through her to impact the lives of others. And she's a great example of how God can and often does use our efforts to build deeper friendships and to initiate richer conversations with the people in our lives.

THE POWER IN SERVING SELFLESSLY

It was the middle of the pandemic. Nobody had seen anything like it before. People were becoming ill, rapidly declining, landing in the hospital, and often dying there. And the sickness was quickly spreading to others who had been around them.

What's worse, this novel virus was so little understood that when someone did get sick, their friends and family members were discouraged from even visiting them. This was based on the fear that they, too, would somehow contract the illness and end up on their own deathbed—perhaps next to the loved one they had visited.

How did this illness spread? Was it by simple touch? Was it in the air? Was it passed through bodily fluids? At the beginning no one really knew, so everyone was cautioned to play it safe and stay clear of anyone who might be infected. As a result, many who were ill were left to suffer in isolation, and they often spent their final days alone.

In the midst of this horrific situation a man named Roy contracted the disease. Soon, like so many others, he was languishing by himself, with almost none of his friends willing to take the risk of coming to see him. But a rare exception was Pat, a man Roy had gotten to know years earlier. Pat and his wife were committed Christians, and despite the highly publicized dangers of this disease, they felt compelled to visit Roy.

Throwing caution to the wind, they came to stand by Roy's bed. They were there to love, encourage, and serve him in any way they could—including, as prescribed in James 5:14, by anointing him with oil and praying for him.

Roy was moved by their love and concern, as well as by their willingness to sacrifice their own safety on his behalf. And although he wasn't known as a religious person, he was quite open to hearing what Pat Boone and his wife Shirley, as well as several other Christians who visited him around that time, shared about God's salvation.

In fact, it was through these visits and interactions that Roy Fitzgerald, who was much better known by his Hollywood screen name—Rock Hudson—prayed to receive Christ. Only a day or so later, this world-renowned actor died of the horrific pandemic—not Covid-19, but rather the pandemic of that era, HIV/AIDS.

"We all wept afterwards," Pat reported years later. And, based on Roy's receptivity and response to the gospel, Pat concluded, "he went to be with the Lord. AIDS had ruined his normal physical body, but now the Bible says we're given new bodies—eternal bodies. And now we believe that Roy . . . is there with the Lord and he'll welcome us when we come to our eternal habitations." The selfless actions of Pat, Shirley, and several other followers of Christ served to open this legendary actor to the God who loved him more than any of us ever could.

As I mentioned at the end of the last session, I'd urge you to read chapters 3 and 4 of the *Contagious Faith* book before your group meets again. You'll find information and additional stories there that I think will encourage you further in your efforts to build redemptive relationships, and to serve people in ways that model the love and truth of Jesus.

 ## Reflection Questions

1. It would be easy to assume that someone as shy as Julie would not be cut out for evangelism, yet look how God used her! In light of her example, what limitations do you need to overcome in order to have a maximum spiritual impact? What will you do about it?

2. What relational connection do you need to make this week in order to get closer to someone you might influence for Christ? Can you take a tangible step toward making that happen right away?

3. The Rock Hudson story shows that what starts with the giving of tangible help can lead to the quenching of spiritual thirst. Acts of loving service can prompt decisions to follow the loving Savior. Is there someone you sense God leading you to serve? Are you willing to take a risk like Pat and Shirley Boone did?

4. Regardless of how the other person responds, God will be pleased with sacrificial service done in the name of Jesus. When you serve that way, I think he'd say to you what Paul said to the believers in Corinth: *"Therefore, my dear brothers and sisters, stand firm. Let nothing move you. Always give yourselves fully to the work of the Lord, because you know that your labor in the Lord is not in vain"* (1 Corinthians 15:58). Meditate on that promise, and let God use it to motivate you to serve others.

TELLING YOUR FAITH STORY IN A NATURAL WAY

*We proclaim to you what we have seen and heard,
so that you also may have fellowship with us. And our fellowship
is with the Father and with his Son, Jesus Christ.*

1 JOHN 1:3

 Getting Started

Welcome back for session three! Today we're diving into the topic of how we can all talk about our story of finding faith in Christ, as well as the third of the five *Contagious Faith Styles*—the *Story-Sharing* style. But first, let's interact on some of what we discussed in the last couple of sessions as well as the between-sessions activities you've been doing.

Since we discussed the first two topics in some depth—building friendships with unbelievers and serving them in selfless ways—I'd be interested in hearing if any of you had a chance to put either of these approaches into practice. How did it go? Any other plans for what you might do in these areas?

After this session, we'll already be halfway through this training. So let me urge you to keep praying, keep preparing, and keep looking for opportunities to build bridges of friendship and to serve those around you. If you do these things, I think you'll be surprised to see how quickly doors of spiritual conversations can open. Remember that God has been preparing people for what you have to offer as you share his love and truth with them.

Opening Discussion

In his book *Come Before Winter*, Charles Swindoll points out that the apostle Paul stood alone six different times in speaking to often-hostile audiences between his third missionary journey and his trip to Rome (see Acts 22–26).

"Do you know the method Paul used each time?" Swindoll asks. "His personal testimony . . . he simply shared how his own life had been changed by the invasion of Christ and the indwelling of his power."

Why did Paul use this approach? "Because one of the most convincing, unanswerable arguments on earth regarding Christianity is one's personal experience with the Lord Jesus Christ," Swindoll continues. "No persuasive technique will ever take the place of your personal testimony. . . . The skeptic may deny your doctrine or attack your church but he cannot honestly ignore the fact that your life has been changed."[1]

- That's why we're focusing on our faith stories today. We'll look at how we can formulate and share them in ways that will help us reach the people we've been praying for. Perhaps part of what God used to reach you was someone's story of coming to faith in Christ. If that was the case, who was that person and what story did he or she share?

- If, based on the assessment from session one and your reading and interactions since then, you think the *Story-Sharing* style is your primary approach, please raise your hand. Have you had the opportunity to tell your faith story in

---

1. Charles R. Swindoll, *Come Before Winter* (Portland: Multnomah Press, 1985), 43.

situations where you think God used it in someone's life? If so, what happened?

Video Teaching

Now let's watch the teaching video for this session (the streaming video access information is provided on the inside front cover). As you watch, write down any thoughts you'd like to remember.

Main Teaching

In this session, we're going to talk about how we can tell our story in natural ways that God can really use. When I think of faith stories, or testimonies, I automatically think of my buddy, Lee Strobel. You might know of Lee through his books, especially *The Case for Christ*, which more recently was turned into a movie.

Lee was a skeptic and atheist who investigated the Christian faith after his wife, Leslie, suddenly announced she'd become a Christian. His quest lasted almost two years, when he finally reached the point where the evidence compelled him to put his trust in Christ.

As Lee's friend and ministry partner over the years, I've seen how God uses his *Story-Telling* style of evangelism. There are a lot of exciting accounts, as many people have come to faith through hearing Lee's story. There is power in this approach, whether or not your story is dramatic.

Our biblical example of the *Story-Sharing* style is the blind man who Jesus healed in John 9. The man barely had a chance to blink before the religious leaders started challenging him about what happened. He told them his simple but powerful story, which pointed them back to Jesus.

In his own way, Jesus used the *Story-Sharing* style as well—by speaking out of his own experiences in ways that pointed people to the truth of his message, and to the salvation that is available through him alone.

For some of us, the *Story-Sharing* style is our main approach. Those with this style tend to be good storytellers. When you talk about what you did during the summer or even over the weekend, people are interested. And if you'd talk about your *spiritual* experience—especially the details of how you met Christ—they'll probably be interested in that as well.

As followers of Christ all of us have a story to tell, so we'll work on shaping and telling our stories later in this session. For now, though, here are three *Key Skills* that are important for all of us—regardless of what our main *Contagious Faith Style* happens to be.

1. **Use questions to draw out your friend's spiritual beliefs** (find out their story before you try to tell them about yours).

2. **Communicate your story around a natural outline** (here's a framework around three words that start with the letter D):

Discovery – What did you discover spiritually along the way (whether at a young age or more recently, and whether all at once or through a process)?

Decision – What did you do with the information you discovered? There may have been a series of decisions along the way, but ultimately you'll want to talk about how you turned from your old patterns and put your faith in Christ.

Difference – What has changed in your life as a result of knowing Jesus? Without overstating things, how is your life better now with his leadership and forgiveness?

3. **Relate your story to your friend's situation** (focus on the parts of your story that will be most relevant to your friends and their experience, because this is primarily about them.)

Interview

Now let's meet the person we have been talking about during this session: author and pastor Lee Strobel. We want to learn more about his experience with the *Story-Sharing* style, as well as any encouragement he'd like to share about how all of us can talk to others regarding our journey with Christ.

Video Wrap

I hope you were encouraged by hearing a few of Lee's *Story-Sharing* adventures and that both his example and the things we covered in the teaching time inspired you to get ready to share your own story with the people around you—telling them about what you *Discovered* and *Decided* spiritually, and the *Difference* it has made in your life.

Group Interaction

- Before we work on our stories, do you have any quick reactions to what you just heard in the teaching video or through the interview with Lee Strobel?

- I explained that your story doesn't have to be dramatic to be effective and useful in God's hands. Have you ever thought about that before—that maybe your relatively ordinary story of coming to faith in Christ will actually relate better to ordinary people in your life?

Now I want to give you some time to reflect on how you came to faith by focusing on the three areas I talked about in the video: *Discovery, Decision,* and *Difference.* Here they are. Let's take a few minutes to write down some thoughts under each of the following areas.

- **Discovery** — What did you learn that helped you eventually reach the conclusion that you needed Christ and the salvation he offers? Was it when you were a child? Was it a process (it usually is)—or maybe a series of discoveries? Who or what were the main influences on your thinking? Were you immediately open, or was it a more gradual journey? Make some notes below about your spiritual discovery process:

- **Decision** — Describe what you eventually decided to do, based on what you had discovered, as mentioned above. It might be a series of decisions (for example, to search more deeply, to attend a discussion group or church service, or to talk to someone about your spiritual questions.). But be sure to include the ultimate decision you made to ask God for his forgiveness and leadership in your life, based on Jesus' payment on the cross for your sins. Also, try to explain what you did in terms that your friend could imitate, by being specific about what you understood, decided, prayed, etc. Make a few notes below about the details of your decision:

• **Difference** — One of the most important aspects of our spiritual story—especially for friends who are deciding whether or not to follow Christ—is the difference he has made in your life. What are the benefits of knowing him? Be careful. Don't describe the Christian life in rosy or overblown terms, promising something the Bible doesn't promise. But, yes, explain how following Jesus is better. He promised he would give rest to the weary, and in John 10:10 he said he came so that we "may have life, and have it to the full." How has that been true for you? Paint a positive but realistic picture, based on your real experience. Write down some thoughts about how you might do this:

 Group Activity

Now that you've taken some time to consider and write down a few notes detailing your spiritual *Discovery, Decision,* and *Difference* process, briefly review them and highlight a few main points. Then we're going to give you a chance to tell your story to one other person in the group. [Feel free to glance at your notes as needed while practicing. You're still getting to know your story in this format!]

Pair up with someone else—preferably somebody other than your spouse or a longtime friend. Then go ahead and take 3 or 4 minutes each to tell the other person the story about your journey to Christ, following the three-part outline. (NOTE: Have someone let the group know when 4 minutes is up, so the other person can then, in turn, share their story. Then announce again when an additional 4 minutes is up.)

[NOTE: If anyone in your group has not clearly made the decision to follow Christ, they can still talk about their spiritual journey thus far, as well as where they think it might lead next. Better yet, they can pray to receive the forgiveness and leadership of Jesus right now, with the encouragement and support of your circle of loving Christian friends cheering them on!]

❏ How did the practice time go? Did you enjoy talking about God's activity in your life? (Most people find it really encouraging to recount what God has done for them.)

❏ Is there something you would do differently next time you tell your story? (Remember what you'd change, so you can do so this week if you get the chance to share it with someone else!)

❏ Did any of you make a decision today to take next steps in your own spiritual journey? Would you be willing to tell the group about it?

❏ If you have time, would you or someone in the group like to briefly share your story with everyone?

[NOTE: Another great option, if you have some extra time, is to have everyone pair up with a different person and tell your stories to each other again. You'll find your confidence in talking about your testimony will go up exponentially with multiple practices!]

 # Conclusion

As followers of Christ, we continue to *discover* more about God and his will for us, and as we *decide* to obey and follow him, we see more and more positive *differences* in our lives. So, we actually have a number of stories within our broader testimony, and we can draw from these as needed to best relate our experiences to the person we're trying to reach.

But that said, the ultimate *Discovery, Decision, Difference* story that we need to explain is the one related to our having found salvation through Christ.

 # Closing Challenge

This week, try to tell at least one other person your story of spiritual *Discovery, Decision,* and the *Difference* it has made in your life—and then let's hear some reports about how it went at the beginning of the next session!

Don't underestimate how God might use your testimony—especially if you have the *Story-Sharing Contagious Faith Style*. Also, don't be intimidated when you share it with a friend and they say, "That's great—for you. I don't think it's for me, but I'm glad you found what you found." You can gently reply that it's based on what Jesus did for *all* of us, so if it's true for you, then it's true for them too. Urge them to look into it further, keeping their mind open to what God might want to do in their life.

Be sure and dive into the *Between-Sessions Personal Study* materials at the end of this section of the study guide before we meet again. Also, read chapter 5 in the *Contagious Faith* book, where you'll learn more about the ins and outs of sharing our spiritual stories.

Finishing the Session

As you close, pray together as a group for opportunities to share your spiritual stories with more people this week, and for the courage to make the most of those opportunities. Also, ask God to continue to work in the hearts and lives of the people on your prayer list, drawing them to himself for salvation and new life in Christ.

BETWEEN-SESSIONS PERSONAL STUDY

Let's deepen our understanding of what we discussed in our last session by delving into the testimony of the apostle Paul, as he presents his story using the three-part outline that I unpacked in the teaching video.

📖 Section One: Study and Reflect

To make the most of the following study, read Acts 26 in its entirety. It will give you the big picture of what Paul faced that day when he, a prisoner, was assured by King Agrippa in verse 1, "You have permission to speak for yourself." Paul responded by telling his story in a way that naturally flowed with the *Discovery, Decision,* and *Difference* format we've been discussing.

Paul Makes a Discovery: In verses 9–18, Paul described what his life was like before meeting Jesus. He was a persecutor of the church who thought he was serving God by trying to wipe out this fledgling movement of fervent Christ followers.

- How does Paul describe the astounding discovery he made on his journey to Damascus?

- The discovery Paul made that day shook the foundations of most of what he believed and was trying to do in his life. Yet he was willing to follow what he discovered anyway. Were there things you had to change or give up to follow Jesus? Was it worth it? Explain.

- Do you sense that there is more God wants to change in your life as you seek to follow him? Are you willing to trust and obey what he's telling you? Why or why not?

Paul Makes a Decision: In the next verse, Acts 26:19, Paul explained, "So then, King Agrippa, I was not disobedient to the vision from heaven." That's an understated description of the life-changing decision Paul made to not only trust in Jesus for salvation but also to stop persecuting the church and, instead, become a leader in spreading the gospel throughout the world!

- Paul's story reminds us that God knows how to get our attention when he wants to! Did God need to do something in your life to get your attention? In what way?

- Are there people in your life who seem to need a wakeup from God so they'll begin to take him and his offer of salvation seriously? How can you pray for them to that end?

Paul's Life Exhibits a Difference: Verses 20–23 describe how dramatically different Paul's life and mission soon became.

- It is startling to see how quickly Paul turned from a persecutor of the church to a missionary for the church. Also, Acts 9:18 mentions that after Ananias prayed for Paul, "he got up and was baptized." That's the kind of step many people weigh for months or even years before taking action. Is there a next step of obedience God is calling you to take that Paul's example might inspire you to act on now? What is it?

- Our goal should not be to do exactly what Paul did or to try to become clones of the Christians we admire. Rather, we need to find our own God-given gifts and calling. That said, are there steps of obedience to God that these people inspire you to take?

- As you prayerfully consider your answer to the last question, what kinds of actions will you take as a result? Is there a Christian confidant with whom you should share this plan in order to gain their encouragement and accountability?

 ## Section Two: Put It into Practice

As you seek to tell others about the ways that God has worked in your life (and continues to work in you), consider the following cautions.

Cautions Related to Telling Your Faith Story

Embrace Your Story.
Don't underestimate the value of your testimony because it doesn't seem to be dramatic or exciting enough. The examples of skeptics finding faith and blind men being given their sight are thrilling, but not typical. More often our stories are more ordinary—as is mine.

The account of a life turned from sin to the Savior is always significant, but it's not necessarily enthralling. Dramatic stories relate well to certain groups of people, but mine—and maybe yours—resonates with those who have a formal religious background but who haven't really opened themselves up to the forgiveness and leadership of Christ.

Every testimony has an important role in building God's kingdom. Every changed life is a miracle. It's important for each of us to think through how we can effectively organize and articulate our stories and then share them until it feels natural. And for some Christians, perhaps including you, this—the *Story-Sharing* style—will be their primary approach to sharing the Good News with others.

Be Honest.

A second caution is to be honest and realistic about the details of your life. You probably weren't the worst person on the planet before you found God, and your life certainly isn't perfect now. Resist the temptation to overstate either side of that equation. Be honest about your personal ups and downs—both then and now. Also, ask the Holy Spirit, as well as mature believers in your life, for wisdom about which details of your experience are worth mentioning versus ones it would be better to skip. And make sure whatever is shared will ultimately point people back to Christ, and that it will honor him and his work in you.

Tailor to Your Audience.

Even though this is your story, the point of it is to help the person you're sharing it with; it's to use your experience to assist them in understanding how God could work in *their* life. Let that priority be a guiding principle in deciding what to talk about, how much to say, and what to emphasize. Your testimony is multifaceted, and parts of it will connect better with some people than with others. The goal of sharing at least sections of it is to encourage whoever you're talking with to move forward with Christ in ways that reflect your experience with him.

Speak in Plain English.

Don't try to impress people with lofty theological terminology. And maybe even more important: avoid religious clichés and church jargon.

At best, you'll sound like you're from a different world. At worst, you'll be completely misunderstood. In Colossians 4:5–6, Paul warns us to act with wisdom toward outsiders, and to let our "conversation be always full of grace, seasoned with salt, so that you may know how to answer everyone."

So be gracious in how you communicate—but in addition to that, *talk normally*. This, by the way, is a problem that we all struggle with at times. Something practical we can do to improve in this area is to invite Christian friends to tell us when we're speaking in unclear or ineffective ways—and be ready to do the same for them. As Solomon said, "Iron sharpens iron" (Proverbs 27:17), so with each other's help we can all get better at expressing ourselves in ways that are understandable and effective.

 ## Section Three: Reflect on a Key Story

The following is an inspiring story from Lee Strobel that I recount in the *Contagious Faith* book. Take a couple minutes to read it, and then reflect on the questions that follow.

THE POWER OF A FAITH STORY

Robert was known for living on the edge, taking insane risks, and repeatedly dodging death. His success made him wealthy, but he gambled much of his money away. He once went to jail after trying to settle a dispute by using a baseball bat.

At the peak of his success, he owned two private jets, which cost a fortune to fly—but he once ordered both of them into the air at the same time. Why? So he could sip champagne in one of them while looking at his name painted on the side of the other one!

Robert had no interest in God and often ridiculed Christians for their faith. Meanwhile, he lived a lifestyle of habitually breaking many of the Bible's commandments—and this continued until he was sixty-five years old.

Then one day he was out walking when he suddenly sensed God speaking to him. *Robert, I've rescued you more times than you'll ever know*, the inaudible voice said. *Now I want you to come to me through my Son Jesus.*

He was astounded. Why would God talk to him? And what was he supposed to do about it? Robert called one of the few Christians he knew and asked for advice. That friend urged him to read Lee Strobel's book *The Case for Christ*, which he did. The Holy Spirit used Lee's story, along with the evidence that had persuaded Lee to move from atheism to faith.

"All of a sudden I just believed in Jesus Christ. I did! I believed in him!" Robert later recounted. "I just got on my knees and prayed that God would put his arms around me and never, ever, ever let me go."

Robert's life changed radically. Soon, he was sharing his faith with whoever would listen. But he wanted the whole world to know, so he reached out to the pastor of a large church and asked him to baptize him on his televised broadcast, and to let him share his story briefly. When this happened, Robert shared his story with such simplicity and clarity that God moved powerfully throughout the sanctuary—and when the pastor asked if anyone else wanted to put their trust in Christ and be baptized in the same way, many began responding to the opportunity.

With "Amazing Grace" playing in the background, person after person—many with tears streaming down their cheeks—came to the front of the church to put their trust in Jesus. God moved in a powerful way that day, and by the time it was over, *700 people* had committed their lives to Christ!

Robert later became friends with Strobel after calling to thank him for writing his book. His biggest regret, he told him, was that he hadn't given his life to Jesus earlier. He challenged him, saying, "Lee, you have to tell people, 'Don't put this off! *Don't* put it off!'"

"There's just so much I want to do for God," he said again and again.

But time was running out for Robert. He was suffering from a lung condition that took his life just a few months later. When they held his funeral at his hometown in Montana, thousands showed up for it.

"Why would so many people want to honor a guy like Robert?" Strobel later wrote in *The Unexpected Adventure*. "That's a natural question to ask, but only because I haven't told you the rest of the story. You see, nobody called Robert by his real name; they always referred to him instead by his nickname, which was *Evel*."

This unlikely Christian, known by the name *Evel Knievel*, risked his life to jump motorcycles over increasingly challenging obstacles, in the process landing in the *Guinness World Records* book for breaking more bones than any other human being. Unexpectedly, extraordinarily, this once self-absorbed celebrity had been humbled and awed by God's undeserved love.

So while thousands of admirers flocked to his memorial service to pay tribute to Evel, his tribute went somewhere else. Before he died, Evel had asked for these words to be etched on his tombstone for all the world to see: *Believe in Jesus Christ.*

Between now and when your group meets for session four, I recommend reading chapter 5 of the *Contagious Faith* book for more encouragement and to hear additional ways God can use our stories to reach our friends who need to know Christ.

? Reflection Questions

1. The more you learn about the life of Robert—Evel Knievel—the more you'll realize what an unlikely candidate he was for becoming a Christ follower. Yet his story dramatically changed, and then was used to impact many other people. Are there unlikely candidates in your life who, truth be told, you've spiritually written off? How does Robert's story affect that attitude? What can you do to reach out to one of those "candidates"?

2. God used Lee Strobel's story to radically impact Evel Knievel's story. Whose story might God impact through yours? Can you take steps to share it with that person soon? When and where?

3. Evel Knievel's story was used to reach some 700 people at the church the weekend he shared it, and probably many others on the television broadcast that went out from that church. But it was a bold move for him to share it in such a public forum—especially when he'd only been a believer for a few weeks. Have you been limiting how God is able to use you by being too cautious or hesitant to share what he's done in your life? Are there bold moves he is nudging you to take? What will you do?

OFFERING REASONS FOR YOUR FAITH

But in your hearts revere Christ as Lord. Always be prepared to give an answer to everyone who asks you to give the reason for the hope that you have. But do this with gentleness and respect.

— 1 PETER 3:15

 ## Getting Started

Welcome back for session four of the *Contagious Faith* course. In this session we're going to talk about the important matter of how we can offer evidence and solid answers to friends who question the validity of the Christian faith, and we'll unpack the related *Contagious Faith Style*—namely, the *Reason-Giving* approach.

But first, let's take a few minutes to hear stories about any interactions you might have had this past week using any of the other approaches we've been discussing, especially the most recent topic of how we can talk about our journey toward meeting Christ. Did you have a chance to share your faith story with someone? How did it go? Any other opportunities or encounters to mention?

Opening Discussion

"We demolish arguments and every pretension that sets itself up against the knowledge of God," wrote the apostle Paul in 2 Corinthians 10:5. "And we take captive every thought to make it obedient to Christ." This seems like a really intense way of talking about our faith, but there has never been a greater need for this approach than there is right now. Our culture is drifting further and further away from the true God and the Christian worldview. Many people simply don't believe what they used to believe.

It wasn't that long ago, at least here in the West, when almost everyone had some kind of religious training—whether through Sunday school, catechism, parochial school, or vacation Bible school. If you told them they needed Christ, they would probably acknowledge that to be true but add that they weren't ready to follow him just yet. By contrast, a lot of people today want to know how we can be sure God even exists at all, and, if he does, that Jesus was his Son. Many are now convinced that Jesus was just a good moral teacher—one who was completely misunderstood.

As people experience growing levels of confusion about spiritual matters and they raise increasing numbers of objections to the Christian faith, we'll need more and more of us to be prepared to offer evidence and reasons for what we believe. And taking it a step further, some of us were made to specialize in the *Reason-Giving* style of evangelism.

- Did you face intellectual questions or doubts in your own journey toward Christ? What were your main issues, and how did you find answers?

- Do you know someone who is struggling through such questions? What are you doing to help them get the information they need—or what *could* you do?

- Would you say that the *Reason-Giving* style is your main approach? Does anyone else in the group think this is their main approach too, or at least a secondary one?

I would urge you to take note of who has which of these five styles as we go through these discussions together. Then prayerfully consider ways that you can partner with each other to add your strengths in situations where others are weak, so that together you can take steps to reach out to all your friends.

Video Teaching

Now watch the video for session four (streaming video access information is on the inside front cover). As you watch, use the following outline to jot down any concepts that stand out to you.

Main Teaching

I'm excited about this session because I get to talk about my style (and maybe *yours*), as well as the broader topic of giving reasons and answers for our faith.

I came to Christ when I was nineteen. I went to college in my hometown and lived with my parents. I made a deal with my mom. I said, "If the doorbell rings and someone's selling something, that's *your* department. But if they're from a religious group, then *I'll* talk to them."

The doorbell rang a lot. I met people from different religious groups, especially Mormons and Jehovah's Witnesses, and we had great conversations. Around that time I also met a Bahá'í, Muslims, Wiccans, agnostics, and atheists. God had me in the school of hard knocks!

My main approach is the *Reason-Giving* style. I hope it's many of yours as well because it's such an important one, especially in our increasingly secular and skeptical culture. People need answers. They need reasons. They need to know that what we believe makes sense and that we're not taking a blind leap of faith. We have reasons for what we believe.

Our biblical example for the *Reason-Giving* style is the apostle Paul, in Acts 17, when he was talking to a bunch of philosophers in Athens, Greece. He used their idol with the inscription "To an Unknown God" to tell them about the real God. After a few interactions, several of those thinkers ended up becoming followers of Christ.

This style fit Jesus as well. He often gave evidence and reasons for believing in him. He didn't tell people to have blind faith or to simply accept him. He'd say things like, *If you don't believe my words, check out my works—you know, the miracles that I'm doing. They attest to who I am.*

This may be your main approach as well. What's a description of someone who's natural with the *Reason-Giving* style? Well, you like to research things. You've got to know what's true and how it works. You're logical. You're analytical. You like to debate ideas, and you always want to have reasons and evidence to back up what you say.

This approach is increasingly important in our culture because people are raising more and more doubts and questions. They don't easily accept ideas just because a preacher said it or a book teaches it. They want to know, *Are there reasons?* The good news is we have solid reasons and evidence to give them.

Let's look at three *Key Skills* in this area that relate to all of us. I'm drawing these from 1 Peter 3:15, where Peter says, "But in your hearts revere Christ as Lord. Always be prepared to give an answer to everyone who asks you to give the reason for the hope that you have. But do this with gentleness and respect."

1. **Be Prepared to Give Sound Answers and Evidence:** All of us need to be ready, according to Peter, to give an answer. We all need to prepare for this. To study up. Because people ask hard questions these days!

2. **Respond to Questions with Gentleness and Respect:** When we're answering someone's questions or objections to what we believe, our attitude and approach is important. As the end of 1 Peter 3:15 explains, gentleness and respect are vital. These attributes will be

attractive to your friends and help them keep an open mind as they consider what they're hearing.

3. **Move from Good Answers to the Good News:** We need to discern how much information to give before getting back to our central message. Your goal is not just to win arguments; it's to win people to Jesus. Looking again at 1 Peter 3:15, you should be ready to give reasons "for the hope that you have." That's more than general evidence—that's the Good News of the gospel.

Interview

Now let's go to an interview I did with a friend who exemplifies the approach we've been discussing. Alisa Childers was once known for singing in a Christian touring group called ZOEgirl, but more recently she has developed the *Reason-Giving* style, which she expresses in her video podcasts as well as in her excellent book, *Another Gospel?*

Video Wrap

I hope you were encouraged by Alisa's words and example. I know I was. I've seen over and over how giving good answers can help remove intellectual roadblocks and clear the pathway back to the gospel and our friend's need for the Savior.

So let me encourage you: If this is your style, then really go for it. Begin to study and seriously work on this. But for all of us, let's take a few steps to get ready to answer people's questions.

 Group Interaction

- In light of what we just heard, what were your reactions to the lessons in the video or the interview with Alisa Childers?

- Have any of you faced the kinds of faith challenges that I described encountering earlier in my life? How did you respond? Did it compel you to study and find answers, or did you find yourself simply avoiding the issues altogether? If the latter, do you feel motivated to take another look into the answers to those objections? I hope so!

- I mentioned several books and resources that might be helpful in these areas (and there are a wealth of them listed in the "Recommended Resources" section in the back of this study guide). Are there any books, blogs, or broadcasts that you've found especially helpful? If so, which ones, and why?

Now let's read and reflect on a few of the most common objections people bring up concerning our faith, which I mentioned in the video. These questions, along with short answers, are distilled from my book, *The Questions Christians Hope No One Will Ask (With Answers)*, where I deal with these five issues along with five additional ones.

Here's what I'd like you to do: Scan all five of the questions and choose the one you think you're most likely to encounter, and then take a few minutes to review the answer I've provided. Highlight any parts you'd like to remember and write down any additional thoughts that might be helpful in answering that question. [NOTE: This will probably take about 6 or 8 minutes. Go ahead and do this, and then I'll give instructions for how we'll try out our answers.]

"What makes you so sure that God exists at all—especially when you can't see, hear, or touch him?"

[Short answer: We believe in many things we can't see or touch— like love, hope, and justice. And oxygen! We can confidently believe in God based on our experience of him, as well as the evidence related to the beginning of the universe (most scientists believe it sprang into existence out of nothing in a fraction of a second, which squares with Genesis 1:1), the design that is evident throughout creation (including the astonishing ways the cosmos is fine-tuned to support life), and the reality of objective moral standards by which humans know right and wrong. In addition, we have the historical record of God intervening in human history in miraculous ways, and especially through Jesus—the long-awaited Messiah who proved he was the Son of God by predicting his own death and resurrection, and then fulfilled what he said.]

"Why trust the Bible, a book based on myths and full of contradictions and mistakes?"

[Short answer: People with a bias against the idea of miracles call accounts of God's miraculous activity *myths* because they rule out anything supernatural, often without even examining the evidence. Also, most of what they call contradictions or mistakes in the Bible are really just differences in the perspectives and degree of details reported by the various eyewitnesses to the events. The Bible has remarkable historical accuracy and consistency; it includes scores of prophecies that have been fulfilled against all odds; it has been repeatedly confirmed through an abundance of archaeological evidence; and it demonstrates remarkable insight into the human heart and condition. In short, it reads like what it is—a revelation from God.]

"Everyone knows that Jesus was a good man and a wise teacher—but why try to make him into the Son of God, too?"

[Short answer: The early biographies of Jesus—the Gospels—make it clear that Jesus was the Son of God. In fact, the most popular verse in the Bible, John 3:16, says "God so loved the world that he gave *his one and only Son,* that whoever believes in him shall not perish but have eternal life" (emphasis mine). And Jesus made Peter's confession that Jesus was "the Son of the living God" a bedrock teaching of the church (Matthew 16:16–17). Also, this objection overlooks the historical evidence that Jesus fulfilled numerous Old Testament messianic prophecies, that he did a variety of miracles in the presence of even hostile eyewitnesses, that he described himself in divine terms and willingly received worship, and that he proved it was all true by rising from the dead (see Acts 2:22–24).]

"How could a good God allow so much evil, pain, and suffering—or does he simply not care?"

[Short answer: The biblical worldview tells us we live in a fallen world in which, as Jesus explains, "you *will* have trouble" (John 16:33, emphasis mine), and where God allows us the freedom to obey or turn away from him (because real love always entails the ability not to love; see Joshua 24:15). Humanity's sins brought evil and suffering into the world, but God promises to walk with his people through every valley—"but take heart! I have overcome the world" (John 16:33; Matthew 28:20; Psalm 23), and his justice will finally prevail (see Revelation 20:11–15). He promises us as his followers to bring good out of everything we experience (see Romans 8:28). *And, yes, God cares about us and our suffering*—enough to send his Son, who "suffered once for sins, the righteous for the unrighteous, to bring you to God" (1 Peter 3:18).]

"Why should I think that heaven really exists—and that God sends people to hell?"

[Short answer: We have thousands of accounts of near-death experiences by people around the world that testify to the reality of the afterlife—often with details that are virtually impossible to explain in any other way. But our best evidence is the testimony of Jesus, who came from heaven, and who assures us heaven is the ultimate home of all who trust and follow him (see John 3:13; John 14:1–4). Also, God doesn't send anyone to hell. He sent his Son to die for our sins in order to open the gates of heaven to everyone (see John 3:16), but we must receive the offer of the gospel (see John 1:12) or pay the penalty for our own sins (see Romans 6:23). The choice—and the responsibility—is ours (see Revelation 22:17).]

 ## Group Activity

Now that you've taken time to choose a question and prepare a response, we're going to give you a chance to try answering it with another person in your group. If possible, find someone who focused on a different question than you did, and pair up with them to practice. Specifically, show them which question you're going to answer, let them ask you that question, and then take 3–4 minutes to answer it. [NOTE: It's fine to look at the notes you've written or highlighted for this question while you answer it.] After you're done giving your response, see if your answer made sense to them, or if you need to try and clarify anything.

Now reverse roles, with you asking the other person their chosen question, and let them give you the answer they've prepared.

[NOTE: Don't feel bad if you sense you're a bit out of your league. This may be new to you, and it will take further study and practice to get more comfortable—but this was an important first step.]

If time allows, add this exercise: Take turns trying to answer the question your practice partner just answered, and then let them do the same. You can help each other out as needed, but this will be a good way to start getting prepared to answer a second question. (Also, in the between-session exercises we'll give you a chance to work on all five of these questions.)

❑ How did the practice time go? Do you feel at least a little more prepared to "give an answer to anyone who asks you" that particular question?

❑ Do you feel inspired to study these kinds of questions further? Any ideas for next steps you might take in the next few days to become better prepared with answers?

☑ Conclusion

These are challenging questions, to be sure. But they, and many others like them, are objections we don't have to be afraid of or shrink back from answering, because what we believe is *true*. No, the answers aren't simple or wrapped neatly in a bow—but they make sense and point to the trustworthiness of our Christian beliefs. And I'm convinced that the more deeply you study them, the more confident of this you'll become, and that you'll begin to see them not as issues to avoid but as entrées into fruitful conversations about the truth of our faith. And for some of you—those with the *Reason-Giving Contagious Faith Style*—this will be your main approach to sharing your faith with the people around you!

 ## Closing Challenge

I want to urge you between now and when we meet again: Pray for opportunities. Look for opportunities. Initiate conversations with people who have different points of view. Ask them questions and find out what they believe and why. In so doing, you'll learn more about them, and you'll earn the right to offer information about what you've discovered in these areas. Then venture your answers, and see how God works through you as you gently and respectfully point them to the truth of Christ. At the beginning of our next session we'll give you the chance to share a story about how it went!

Before then, be sure to engage in the *Between-Sessions Personal Study* materials (in the pages that follow). Also read chapter 6 of the *Contagious Faith* book, where you'll find more ideas and inspiration to help you in answering people's questions and objections.

If you'd like to go further in studying the kinds of issues we've discussed in this section, you might be interested in the Lee Strobel Center for Evangelism and Applied Apologetics. For more information about our online university courses and certificates, see the page about the Strobel Center in the back of this guide.

 ## Finishing the Session

Let's close in prayer, asking God to help us open conversations with people about questions that really matter, and to guide us in giving answers that will help them not only to resolve these issues but also to realize their need for the Savior.

BETWEEN-SESSIONS PERSONAL STUDY

I hope you'll see what we've done in this last session as merely an introduction to a lifetime of study and preparation in these areas. Our culture is trying to ignore or bury this information, but our friends are dying to know it. We need to do all we can to gear up and get ready to talk about it so that we'll be able, as Colossians 4:6 puts it, to "know how to answer everyone."

Section One: Study and Reflect

Because the questions we discussed in this session are so important, our main activity for this between-sessions time will be to study those issues further, in order to "be prepared to give an answer" on all five of them.

Specifically, go back to the pages in the "Group Interaction" section and study each of the short answers I've offered there (including the one you focused on and answered during the session). Highlight any parts that stand out to you as being particularly important and write down additional thoughts on the lines below the answers. Also, if possible, find someone with whom you can practice giving each of the answers, so you'll become really familiar with the information and increasingly comfortable in talking about it.

In addition, using the space below, I'd urge you to write down any other questions outside of the five we've discussed that you think your friends or family might be curious about. Then do a bit of your own research in order to find good answers to those questions. To help you do that, review the "Recommended Resources" section at the back of this study guide—especially the section labeled "Books on Evidence for the Christian Faith," as well as the list of ministry websites at the end.

Section Two: Put It into Practice

As you look for opportunities to talk to people about their spiritual questions, objections, and doubts, consider the following cautions.

Cautions Related to Giving Reasons for Our Faith

Clarify the Question.

Before giving somebody your *reasons*, make sure you really understand their *questions*. Ask them what they believe about spiritual matters, how they arrived at their conclusions, and whether that's what they've always believed. If not, what led them to change their thinking? Are they confident about what they believe now? Do they have reasons that support their opinions, or are they mostly holding on to things they grew up with? Ask, and then really listen. In doing this, you'll know better who you're talking to, and you'll earn the right to offer your thoughts as well.

Study Up.

Do your homework. Peter said to "be prepared" (1 Peter 3:15). It's not enough to have an inclination toward this approach—you must really study. That will take time and energy spent reading and researching, and it will need to be an ongoing effort. There's always more to learn and new objections to address.

Admit It When You Don't Know.

Don't make up answers. When you don't know something (and that will often be the case, especially at the beginning), don't pretend you do. Instead, admit that you haven't read up on that area yet and, if needed, ask the person for more information.

I mentioned in the last video about the time I struck up a conversation with the young lady who was playing her guitar at a shopping mall. As I started talking about my faith in Jesus, she politely informed me that, for her, Jesus was just one of many prophets. She explained that she was a Bahá'í—a member of a worldwide faith community that follows the prophet Bahá'u'lláh.

I had no idea what or who she was talking about. So, I asked her lots of questions—and I went home and researched the topic further. Then I got back to her to share what I had learned, what my concerns were, and why I thought she should consider the biblical gospel over and above what she'd been taught.

You can do the same. *Admit you don't know, ask questions, do research, and come back with good answers.* You'll demonstrate humility, engage the other person, show you care enough to study their beliefs, and provide genuinely helpful information. Plus, you'll learn a lot along the way. Practice this approach consistently over time, and you will have a rapidly growing reservoir of reasons to draw from.

Win People, Not Arguments.

Offer good arguments for your faith, but don't devolve into argumentativeness. As soon as you let emotions get in the way of respectful conversation, you've strayed from the goal. Our purpose is to win *people*, not points. Also, be careful in deciding which issues you're willing to discuss with unbelievers. Hint: that generally should not include trivial differences about obscure Bible verses, peripheral doctrinal issues, in-house denominational disputes, or mere curiosity questions. Debating these matters usually generates more heat than light, and it rarely does anything to move the person toward Christ.

Ask yourself, *Is this really worth discussing? Will it help lead my friend to the Savior—or is it an unnecessary detour?* Then, as much as possible, stick to central issues.

Paul's admonition to Timothy squares with this. "Don't have anything to do with foolish and stupid arguments, because you know they produce quarrels. And the Lord's servant must not be quarrelsome but must be kind to everyone, able to teach, not resentful. Opponents must be gently instructed, in the hope that

God will grant them repentance leading them to a knowledge of the truth" (2 Timothy 2:23–25).

Expect a Little Tension.
Don't back off from presenting the gospel because you're afraid the other person might not like what you say. This is one of our greatest challenges in the church today. A lot of Christians—especially younger ones—think it's unloving to ever disagree with someone's ideas. They've convinced themselves that the highest value in a friendship is to consistently keep things peaceful and harmonious.

I understand the temptation to think that way, but Jesus said following him would sometimes bring division (see Luke 12:51–53). That's not the goal, of course, but the surpassing value of your friends coming to know God makes the possibility of relational ripples well worth the risk. In fact, offering your friends reasons to follow the One who offers salvation is the most loving thing you can do for them.

Speaking from experience, this can cause temporary tension in relationships. But as God works in your friends over time, that tension can be replaced by a spiritual bond that is stronger than anything you might imagine—one that will last for eternity.

Section Three: Reflect on a Key Story

The following is a story about a friend in Chicago that I tell in the *Contagious Faith* book. Take a moment to read it, and then consider your responses to the questions at the end.

THE IMPACT OF GIVING REASONS FOR OUR FAITH

"A Skeptic's Surprise" was a *Reason-Giving* event that we designed to reach out to Jewish people in our community. It was an exciting night, and the speaker's story gave a compelling account of a highly reluctant seeker slowly finding faith in Jesus, his Messiah.

Don Hart, a Jewish businessman, hesitantly attended that event. Upon leaving, Don couldn't get the message out of his mind. Suddenly he was thinking about spiritual questions he'd never considered before. *Could the messianic prophecies in the Old Testament really point to Jesus of Nazareth? Did Jesus really provide evidence that he was the Messiah? Are there solid reasons to believe in Jesus's miracles—especially the resurrection? Could he become a follower of Jesus without losing his Jewish identity?*

Don tracked me down to discuss his concerns. When we met in my office at the church, I immediately sensed his sincerity. He listened intently as I answered his questions. He wrote out many of my responses and jotted down the names of the books I encouraged him to read. Then when we'd get together again, he would have one or two of those books with him, the pages dog-eared and highlighted—and he'd always show up with a fresh set of questions.

Incredibly, after months of meeting and discussing his seemingly endless flow of concerns, everything began to culminate when Don started talking about—*of all things*—attending seminary! At first, I thought he was joking, but then he asked if I would write a letter of recommendation to help him get into a top evangelical graduate school.

"I'd be happy to, Don," I responded, "except I think you've gotten things a bit out of order. Don't you suppose it would be a good idea to become a *Christian* first—*then* consider going to a Christian seminary?"

With a twinkle in his eye, Don admitted there was a certain logic to what I was saying. This led into one more conversation about some of his remaining concerns. Finally, Don acknowledged that he had found satisfactory answers to most of his questions, and with great joy he prayed with me to receive Jesus as his Messiah and Savior.

Don has been living an exciting adventure ever since that day! Though already in his fifties at the time, he did enroll at the seminary, where he rapidly grew in his understanding of God and the Bible. A couple of years later he graduated, and since then he has served as a biblical counselor, encouraging others in *their* spiritual journeys. And occasionally Don even gets to pray with someone to trust in Jesus, just as I had been given the privilege of doing with him.

Whenever I think of Don, I marvel at the importance of giving people reasons to consider the claims of Christ.

Between now and when your group meets for session five, I recommend reading chapter 6 of the *Contagious Faith* book to gain more encouragement and to hear more stories of how God can work through the reasons we give our friends for the validity of the Christian faith.

Reflection Questions

1. I often remind fellow believers that some of their family and friends are just a few good answers away from being ready to trust in Jesus. Does someone come to mind when I say that? Do you know what his or her questions are?

2. Do you feel ready to respond to the issues that friend might raise? What do you need to read, study, watch, or listen to in order to be prepared to answer your friend's questions?

3. What's your next step toward engaging this person in a conversation? Do you need to invite them to your home, or to a coffee shop, or to lunch? Get ready and take that step—and see what God might do through it!

SHARING THE TRUTH
OF THE GOSPEL

*For I am not ashamed of the gospel, because it is the
power of God that brings salvation to everyone who believes:
first to the Jew, then to the Gentile.*

—ROMANS 1:16

 ## Getting Started

Welcome back for session five! I'm excited to dive into the important
subject matter we're addressing in this session. But first let's pause to
find out if you had a chance to talk with anyone about reasons and
evidence that back up your faith, as we discussed last week.

How did it go? Did you feel prepared or did it spur you to study
further—or maybe a little of both? For me, it's usually a mix. Even
though I've been talking with people about their questions and objections for many years, I usually walk away from conversations feeling
happy that I had some helpful answers—but also compelled to go home
and study the matter further.

I think that's going to be true for all of us, but for those of us
with the *Reason-Giving* style, it's a lifelong process. That's okay. It's

a fascinating process that will keep you learning new information as well as help you become more and more prepared to "give an answer to everyone who asks . . ." (1 Peter 3:15).

Opening Discussion

We live in a noncommittal culture. People are simply more hesitant to sign on to things—especially if there's a long-term pledge involved. Fewer people are getting married, and when they do, it's usually at a higher age . . . This is happening in the spiritual arena as well. They might visit a house of worship, but actually join the church? *Going to need to think about that!*

Welcome to a world of fence-sitters. That's why we need truth-tellers. People who will get to the point, explain the message of the gospel, and nudge their listeners to make a decision. To act on what they know to be true.

- I'm not just speaking theoretically. I was a spiritual fence-sitter all through high school. I thank God that about a year after graduation a *Truth-Telling* friend challenged me with the reality of my situation. His nudge got me thinking, and about a week later I gave my life to Christ (you'll hear a bit about it in the teaching video as well as in the *Between-Sessions Personal Study* section). So, believe me, *I thank God* for those of you who have this approach. Can you relate to a time when you needed someone to step up and give you a spiritual nudge? Who was it, and what happened?

- Based on the assessment we took early in this course as well as what you heard in the teaching video, would you say that the *Truth-Telling* approach is your main style? A secondary style?

- Have you employed this approach in ways that God seemed to use? If so, can you briefly tell the group about it?

Video Teaching

Now let's watch the video for this session (see streaming video access information on the inside front cover). As you watch, write down any thoughts you'd like to remember in the spaces below.

Main Teaching

This session is really important because we are talking about truth-telling and how we can get to the gospel message. One of my favorite stories along these lines is from a friend named Greg Stier, who tells about his Uncle Jack, a tough bodybuilder.

A preacher named Yankee went to share Christ with Uncle Jack on a dare from Bob, Jack's friend. Yankee explained the gospel to Jack and his wife, who had never understood it before. At the end of that conversation Jack was ready to respond, and both he and his wife prayed to receive Christ right then and there.

Jack immediately began to tell others about his newfound faith. He soon led a coworker named Thumper to Christ, then another uncle, and over time many more. All of this started to change Greg Stier's broader family—and eventually Greg ended up trusting in Jesus as well.

Also, get this: Greg later started a ministry called Dare 2 Share, and through that he has now trained well over a million high school students to talk to their friends about the gospel!

This illustrates the power of the *Truth-Telling* style. Yankee used it. Jack used it. Greg uses it. And now Greg has trained a generation of students to share their faith in similar ways as well. Talk about *contagious*!

This is a powerful approach, and it's one that you might have. We *need* people who can get to the point and present the gospel clearly!

Our biblical example is the apostle Peter in Jerusalem on the day of Pentecost (see Acts 2). He stands up and in a very direct way tells the crowd the truth of the gospel. And God used it as 3,000 people came to faith that day through the bold, *Truth-Telling* style of Peter!

Jesus was the ultimate truth-teller. He always told people the truth, and he challenged them with the implications of what he was saying. In John 14:6 he declared, "I am the way and the truth and the life. No one comes to the Father except through me." He was saying, *I am the Son of God, so give me the right place in your life.*

Those with this style tend to be bold and direct. You want to get to the point. You don't like a lot of small talk. You like to change things—to create action. And if you'd apply your strong personality to sharing your faith with others, God could use you in a powerful way.

Here are three *Key Skills* that we can all learn related to this approach:

1. **Be Bold in Initiating Spiritual Conversations.**

   Don't get locked into just the first part of "relational evangelism." The *relational* part is important and often helpful, but we have to get to the *evangelism* part, and that requires words. So try to bring up spiritual matters sooner, and see who is interested. You'll be surprised to discover how many people want to talk about it!

2. **Get to the Central Message of the Gospel.**

   There's a point where we need to actually *get to the point* of the gospel, because as Romans 1:16 makes clear, that's where the power is. So how can we explain our central message? Let's review four ways.

   • **The Story of the Gospel.** The first way is to simply explain the story of Jesus, highlighting the main points of the Good News as Paul does in 1 Corinthians 15:3-8, 20-28, where he cites an ancient creed which lists the key elements of the gospel. This is foundational to helping friends understand the big picture of our message. Here's a summary of what's in that passage:

     ▪ Jesus, the Son of God and predicted King, came to our fallen planet
     ▪ he died for our sins
     ▪ he was buried

- he rose on the third day
- he appeared to many witnesses
- he returned to heaven until he comes back to establish his kingdom with us, his followers

This is the essential message that Paul and the other apostles preached, and we can share it with our friends in a conversational way, whether in one talk or over multiple discussions. It forms the biblical framework for all the other illustrations (including the three below).

- **The Faith Formula**, which we draw from John 1:12, shows that coming to Christ entails three elements that make up a simple equation. Here's the verse (emphases mine): "Yet to all who did *receive* him, to those who *believed* in his name, he gave the right *to become* children of God." And here's the equation [NOTE: It's helpful to write out this formula as you talk about it.]:

BELIEVE + RECEIVE = BECOME

This means that we must *believe* the key elements of the gospel (summarized above) but, more than that, we need *to receive* Jesus and his offer of salvation and leadership in our lives. When we do that we *become* a child of God.

- **Do vs. Done** explains that many people are into religion, but religion is spelled D-O [NOTE: It's helpful to write the word "D-O"]. It consists of trying to *do* enough good things to earn our way to God. The problem is that we can never do enough. Romans 3:23 says we all fall short of God's standard.

   Thankfully Christianity is spelled differently. It's spelled D-O-N-E [Add the letters "N-E," so it says "D-O-N-E"]. That means Christ has already done for us what we could never do for ourselves. He lived the perfect life that we could never live, and he died to pay the penalty for our sins. But it's not enough to know this; we need to humbly receive what Christ has done for us by asking him for his forgiveness and leadership in our life.

• **The Bridge** is the final illustration—one that we draw [NOTE: Draw this along with me in the box below]. This one helps people visualize the gospel—as well as what they need to do. It shows that though God created us and wants to have a relationship with us, our sins have separated us from him—and we can't overcome that separation on our own. Worse, our disobedience to God has earned us a spiritual death penalty, which means separation from God for eternity. We're in real trouble!

Thankfully, God *still* loves us and wants to have a relationship with us. That's why he sent Jesus to be "the Bridge" between him and us. How? By dying on the cross to pay the penalty for our sins. Now he offers us the way back to God and his forgiveness. It's not enough to just know this. We must admit our sins and ask him to forgive us and to begin leading our lives. *That's* how we cross over the Bridge and start a new life of following him.

Draw *The Bridge* illustration:

Now let me mention one more important *Key Skill* for this session:

3. Ask People to Respond to the Gospel

We must not stop with simply presenting the message of salvation. We need to give the person a chance to respond to it. So when you sense that your friend is becoming receptive, it's often appropriate to ask, *Is there any reason you wouldn't want to put your trust in Jesus right now?* If they're open, don't delay. Lead them in a prayer in which they tell God they want to: *Turn* from their sins, *Trust* in the Savior, and *Follow* him as their Lord and King. If they take this step, *celebrate* with them!

Interview

Now let's watch a short interview I did with my friend Greg Stier. He's the guy I've been talking about in this session—the one who had a relative named "Uncle Jack," and who later started the Dare 2 Share ministry. Greg is a powerful example of the *Truth-Telling* style—presenting the gospel in clear and compelling ways. If you want more details about his story, check out his new memoir, *Unlikely Fighter: The Story of How a Fatherless Street Kid Overcame Violence, Chaos & Confusion to Become a Radical Christ Follower.*

Video Wrap

I hope you're encouraged by Greg's example. He certainly inspires me! Let me encourage you now to interact with each other and practice some of these things in order to get more confident in sharing the gospel. Then this week look for opportunities to say to people, *You may be curious to know what it is I believe. Can I share this illustration with you? Or can I draw a picture for you that sums it all up?* Just try it and see how God might use it!

 # Group Interaction

- Before we focus on reviewing and trying out some of the gospel presentations, do you have any quick thoughts or

SESSION FIVE | SHARING THE TRUTH OF THE GOSPEL

reactions to what you just heard in the teaching video, including the interview with Greg Stier?

• Many times, the people who see great fruit from their evangelistic efforts are those with the bold *Truth-Telling Contagious Faith Style*. Can you think of any examples that have inspired you? Is there some aspect of what they do that you would like to emulate?

• At the end of the *Key Skills* section, I talked about how we can pray with someone to receive the salvation of Christ, helping them *Turn* from their sins, *Trust* in the Savior, and *Follow* him as their Lord and King. Have you ever had the opportunity to lead someone in a prayer like that? How did it go?

• Now I want to give you some time to review the four approaches I taught in the video—*The Story of the Gospel* as well as the three gospel illustrations (all listed below). Choose the one you think the main person you're trying to reach would best relate to, and read through it, highlighting any key ideas you want to remember. In a few minutes we'll give you a chance to practice sharing it with another person in your group. [NOTE: To review any of the first three, turn back to the outlines in the video teaching section above. For *The Bridge*, see the details on how to draw it below. Allow about 6–8 minutes for this review/preparation time.]

- *The Story of the Gospel,* based on the passage in 1 Corinthians 15
- *The Faith Formula,* based on John 1:12: BELIEVE + RECEIVE = BECOME
- *Do vs. Done,* which contrasts our efforts to D-O enough to earn our way to God, versus trusting in Jesus and what he has D-O-N-E for us
- *The Bridge* illustration, which we draw on a piece of paper to help people visualize the gospel and to see how they can get back over to God

Below you will find a transcript of what I taught on the video when I presented my version of *The Bridge,* along with a step-by-step illustration of the drawing (adapted from *The Bridge,* © 1981, by the Navigators. Used by permission of NavPress. All rights reserved.) You can use this as a rough script of what to say, although it's often a good idea to put it into your own words.

There's a God who created us, loves us, and wants to have a relationship with us. [Write "God" on the right side, and "Us" on the left side.]

Us   *God*

But there's a problem. We sinned against God. We rebelled against him. And when we did, it formed this chasm, a separation between us and God. [Add the two walls of the chasm.]

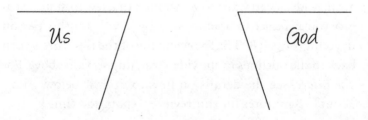

A lot of us think, *I need to earn my way. I need to try harder. I need to do good deeds. I need to get more religious and that will get me back over to God.* But the problem is that those efforts, according to Romans 3:23, fall short of God's holy standard. They always fall over the edge of the chasm. They never get us back to God. [Add a couple of arrows bending over the left side of the chasm, next to "Us."]

And ultimately, because we've sinned and fall short of God's standard, we deserve a spiritual death penalty (Romans 6:23, "the wages of sin is death"). [Write the word "Death" at the bottom of the chasm.]

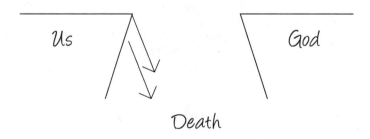

That's the predicament we're in, and that is the *bad news* that shows our need for the gospel. We need to help people understand that we are in trouble. We can't get back to God through our own efforts. But thankfully the God who made us and loved us *still* loves us—enough to send Jesus for us (see John 3:16). Through him and his death for our sins, God built the bridge back to himself that we could not build ourselves. And here's what it looks like. It's not just a bridge across the chasm, but it's the cross of Christ itself. [Draw the cross so it covers the chasm.]

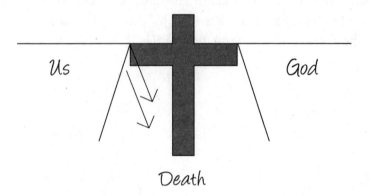

The *Good News* is that Jesus took care of the sin problem that we couldn't. He died so that we would not have to. He paid the death penalty in our place, and he paved the way back to God so that we could know him and become his children. Then he rose from the dead to give us new life. [Cross out the word "Death."]

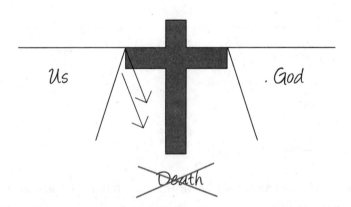

The gospel is Good News, but it's not enough to just know or believe it. We need to *receive* what God offers us. In other words, we're over here on the left side separated from him by our sins. We need to step across to God's side by putting our faith and trust in Jesus. We need to ask him to apply his forgiveness to our lives, to adopt us as his children, and to fill us with his Holy Spirit who will guide us into the future. [Draw the person on the left, an arrow over to God's side, and person over on the right—now forgiven and adopted as a child of God.]

When we take this step and receive Christ, we are forgiven and born anew spiritually. And *that* begins a new adventure of following him.

Draw *The Bridge* illustration:

_____

Group Activity

Now that you've taken time to choose and review a gospel illustration, we're going to give you a chance to present it to another person in your group. Pair up with someone who is ready to share a different illustration from the one you picked—and, if possible, somebody you haven't done a practice session with previously. Then simply take turns explaining (and drawing) the illustrations you chose, taking about 3–4 minutes each.

Here are a few tips for your practice time:

Relax, and enjoy talking about the best Good News anyone has ever heard!

If you're sharing the *Faith Formula*, write out BELIEVE + RECEIVE = BECOME on a piece of paper as you explain each component. If you're sharing the *Do vs. Done* illustration, write the word D-O while talking about how people try to *do* enough to earn their way to God. Then when you get to the message of what Jesus has *done* for us, add the N-E to spell the word D-O-N-E. Or, if you're presenting *The Bridge*, draw the picture in the empty box above (it's after the point-by-point explanation) while talking it through.

Feel free to look at your notes or outline as you practice. This is meant to be a helpful exercise, not a pass/fail examination!

If something your partner is explaining seems a bit unclear, feel free to jump in during the practice and ask for clarification (just as your friends would do if they didn't understand what you're saying to them).

Don't feel bad if it doesn't go as smoothly as you hoped. That's why we're *practicing*—to learn how to do it better and better, so then when you're talking to your friend or family member you'll be as prepared as possible.

[NOTE: Have someone keep time and alert the group when the first 4 minutes have passed, and then again after the second set of 4 minutes.] In addition, if time allows, add a second practice, but this time present the illustration back to your partner that you just heard from them. You can help each other out as needed, but this will be a good way to start getting prepared on a second illustration, and to feel more ready to share the gospel in general.

After practicing your gospel illustration(s) with each other, discuss the following:

❑ How did the practice time go? Do you feel more prepared to explain the gospel to others outside of the group? Is there something you'd do differently next time?

❑ Is there another Christian in your life with whom you could practice your gospel illustration this week? Would you commit to doing so? Trying this again while it's still fresh in your mind will help you grow exponentially in your confidence to share it (and it will begin equipping that person as well)!

❑ Consider the non-believer in your life with whom you'd most like to share the gospel? Are there steps you could take soon to help make that happen? What are they? [If you have a few minutes left before you need to end the group time together, tell the person you just practiced with who that person is and what you think your next step should be. Then pray together, asking God to help you both have those conversations soon.]

Conclusion

We've covered a lot in this session. We've learned about the *Truth-Telling Contagious Faith Style*, and we've discussed several *Key Skills* that will help us communicate the gospel to the people around us. We also practiced explaining a gospel illustration to someone in the group. Now we just need to keep honing what we've learned and prayerfully put it into practice.

 ## Closing Challenge

God can use each of us to share his Good News with our family and friends. More than that, he wants to use us as instruments in their salvation. We can do this with his help. Jesus promised in John 15:5, "If you remain in me and I in you, you will bear much fruit." And he reminded us in the Great Commission (see Matthew 28:18–20) that he will be with us as we go—always.

We just need to bring it up, to explain what people need to believe about God in order to receive the forgiveness and leadership of Christ and to become dearly beloved children of God. Remember: we have great news—now we just need to spread it around.

So, take some risks, and then in the coming days and weeks share some stories with group members, family, and friends about how God is using your efforts!

Also, I'd urge you once again to do the *Between-Sessions Personal Study* and to read chapters 7 and 8 of the *Contagious Faith* book. This will help deepen your understanding of the truth of the gospel and of the varieties of ways we can illustrate it for our friends. You'll also read more stories about how God can use the efforts of ordinary believers—like us!

 ## Finishing the Session

Let's close in prayer, thanking God that he has done everything necessary for our salvation—and for the salvation of our loved ones—and that all we need to do is follow him faithfully and share his Good News with those around us!

BETWEEN-SESSIONS PERSONAL STUDY

It would be hard to overstate the importance of the gospel-related material we covered in this last session. As I've mentioned, Romans 1:16 teaches that the gospel is "the power of God that brings salvation to everyone who believes." So, knowing what the message is and how we can effectively illustrate it for others is a matter of spiritual life and death for the people we talk to. Because of this, I want to build on our discussion about it a bit further.

📖 Section One: Study and Reflect

In the teaching video I gave a brief outline of the story of the gospel, based primarily on Paul's opening verses in 1 Corinthians 15. Because this is so vital, I'm going to give an enhanced version of that information below, drawn from the *Contagious Faith* book. This includes a number of Bible verses from which we draw these points, so you may want to look them up and study them further. After that I'll add two more gospel illustrations from the book that we didn't have time to cover during the session.

I'd urge you to get to know this new material well and, in addition, to go back and review the illustrations we covered during the session. The more familiar you are with this content, the better prepared you'll be to explain the life-giving message of the gospel.

The Story of the Gospel

Here are the main points of the gospel, expanded with a little more explanation as well as several Scripture references that back them up:

- Jesus, the Messiah and Lord (the long-awaited King of Israel and incarnate God of the universe), came to our sinful and fallen planet, bringing God's kingdom (see 1 Corinthians 15:3; Mark 1:15; Acts 2:36).

- King Jesus was rejected and condemned, and he died a criminal's death for us—the spiritual criminals—and for our sins, as predicted (see 1 Corinthians 15:3; Isaiah 53; Philippians 2:8; 1 Peter 3:18).

- Jesus was really dead, and his body was buried in a tomb (see 1 Corinthians 15:3-4).

- Three days later Jesus was raised back to life, as prophesied (see 1 Corinthians 15:4; Isaiah 53:10-12; Psalm 16:9-11; also predicted by Jesus in all four Gospels: Matthew 16:21; Mark 9:30-32; Luke 18:31-34; John 2:19-22). This proved that he was the royal Messiah and divine Son of God, who conquered death.

- The resurrected Jesus appeared to his disciples and many others (see 1 Corinthians 15:5-8), proving he truly was alive again, that he is who he claimed to be, and that he is able to give us new life.

- Jesus ascended into heaven, returning to the Father until he comes back again to bring salvation to his people and judgment to those who reject him, and to establish his kingdom forever (see 1 Corinthians 15:20-28).

The Airplane Illustration

Building on the *Faith Formula* (BELIEVE + RECEIVE = BECOME), or any of the gospel illustrations, here's an approach I often use in explaining how we need to *respond* to the message:

Let's say a family member offers to fly you home for the holidays. It's a great offer, but getting there will require two things. First, you have to *believe* that airplanes fly. You'll never be willing to get on one if you don't believe it will really get you over the mountains, right?

But just believing that airplanes fly won't get you home either. You can be fully confident in the science of flight, even hang around an airport and watch planes take off and land. But it takes more than belief in aviation to get there. You must also *receive* the ticket that was purchased for you and use it to board the airplane that is heading to your town. It's the combination of believing and receiving that allows you to *become* a passenger on that flight which will, as a result, get back home.

It is much the same with Christ. We need to go beyond merely *believing* that Jesus is the Son of God who died on the cross for our sins and who rose to give us life. We must take the next step and trust in him personally, *receiving* him as the forgiver of our sins and the leader of our lives. That is the equivalent of "climbing on board" with Jesus in a way that will ultimately get us home spiritually, where we *become* his forgiven sons and daughters.

Romans 10:9-10

"If you declare with your mouth, 'Jesus is Lord,' and believe in your heart that God raised him from the dead, you will be saved. For it is with your heart that you believe and are justified, and it is with your mouth that you profess your faith and are saved" (Romans 10:9–10).

This passage was a favorite of my late friend Nabeel Qureshi, a former Muslim. In his final book, *No God But One*, he asks "What defines Christianity at its core . . . ?" Then he points to Romans 10:9 and says that we find in it "the entire gospel message formulated as the minimum requirement for saving faith. It has three components: (1) that Jesus died, (2) that he rose from the dead, and (3) that he is God." Nabeel would often sum that up with these three words: *Deity, Death*, and *Resurrection*.

So, Jesus is the God who can save us, the Savior who died for our sins, and the risen Lord who can give us new life. But what are we to do with these truths? Verse 10 tells us to believe them in our heart and profess our trust in them with our mouth (which sounds a lot like the John 1:12 formula of Believe + Receive, but with the added element that we should declare this verbally). When we do so sincerely, according to verse 10, we are *justified* (made right with God) and *saved* (given God's salvation). As if to punctuate this promise, a few verses later we're assured that "everyone who calls on the name of the Lord will be saved" (Romans 10:13).

Section Two: Put It into Practice

Cautions Related to Challenging People with Truth

Seek God's Guidance and Wisdom.

Because of the strength of personality that often goes with those who challenge people with truth, it's important to seek wisdom from God (James 1:5), along with the gentleness and respect that Peter prescribes (1 Peter 3:15). It's also important to heed the biblical admonition to "be quick to listen, slow to speak and slow to become angry" (James 1:19). If you come on too strong or too fast, people will likely become defensive and distrust whatever you say.

So, slow down a bit. Seek the guidance and tempering of the Holy Spirit. Listen first, and once you're confident you understand the person's point of view and have earned their trust, then tell them the truth you think God wants them to hear. Expect that their first response may not be to thoughtfully consider what you've said or to thank you for sharing your wisdom. Even with your best efforts to communicate respectfully, many will resist what you're saying, and some will be offended by it.

Remember that many turned away from the teachings of Jesus, the Son of God himself. The same happened with Peter and with Paul, whose listeners often debated their ideas and, in the end, discarded what they'd heard. Jesus cautioned us that just as people rejected him, they will often reject us.

But not all will reject us. Many are fed up with their hollow lives of endless striving, empty pleasure, or feigned religion. They're looking for something real. They're seeking rest for their souls, and relief from their guilt and moral bankruptcy. They're looking for Jesus and the truth of the gospel—but many of them don't know it yet.

We have the unspeakable privilege of offering it to them—of offering *him* to them. So, under God's guidance, keep patiently reaching out with his love and truth.

Resist Being Overly Cautious.

This leads me to the next concern, which is to resist becoming *overly* cautious. Our culture has become hypersensitive, with many people thinking that the most offensive thing you can do is tell people they're wrong or try to change their mind (as, ironically, they try to tell us *we're* wrong and that we need to change *our* minds). Even among those who identify as Christians, many think it's inappropriate to try to convince someone to change their point of view in order to turn and follow Christ. Yet the kindest thing we can do for our friends is to help them understand there is a loving God who wants to redeem them and renew their lives—*if* they turn to him in repentance and faith.

Look at these penetrating words of atheist Penn Gillette: "If you believe that there's a heaven and a hell . . . how much do you have to hate somebody to *not* proselytize?" As Paul said, *"Christ's love compels us*, because we are convinced that one died for all, and therefore all died. And he died for all, that those who live should no longer live for themselves but for him who died for them and was raised again" (2 Corinthians 5:14–15, emphasis mine).

Our priority, then, should not be to try to keep friendships smooth and tranquil at all costs, or to avoid ever offending anyone. Rather, it should be to "speak the truth in love" (Ephesians 4:15) in order to help secure the salvation and spiritual health of those we care about, even if the truth stings a little in the process. God's love should compel us to tell them about him and his grace, available in Christ.

We shouldn't be afraid, therefore, to occasionally make people feel uncomfortable—it comes with the territory of challenging others with God's truth. Again, don't unnecessarily offend anyone, but be willing to accept some level of uneasiness in others as a by-product of sharing the truth with them. Like Jesus did. And Peter. And Yankee, Uncle Jack, and Greg Stier.

Affirm Different Approaches.

One more word of caution. Once you've developed the courage to challenge people with God's truth, and he has used you to nudge people toward him, be careful not to project that approach onto other Christians, making them feel bad for not exhibiting the same level of boldness as you. Remember there are a variety of approaches to sharing our faith. *You be you*, and *let them be them*, and trust God to use all the members of his body in partnership with each other.

 ## Section Three: Reflect on a Key Story

THE POWER OF THE GOSPEL

I was raised in a Christian home, but when I was nineteen years old, I was not walking with God. I was clearly on the wrong track in my life, seeking fun and adventure, even when it meant coloring outside of the lines morally. I knew what was right, but throughout my high school years and beyond I had resisted it and gone my own way. I needed a spiritual challenge from a *Truth-Telling* friend.

Then one day Terry, a guy I'd known since middle school, entered the electronics shop where I worked. After pretending to be interested in a car stereo, he got to his real point: "So, Mark, are you a Christian?"

His simple question was quite intimidating at the time. "Sure, I'm a Christian, Terry. What about it?" I replied warily.

Terry responded with another question: "How can you call yourself a Christian and yet do so many things that Christians don't do?"

"Well," I said flippantly, "I guess I'm just a *cool* Christian!"

Without batting an eye, Terry shot back, "Oh, really? Don't you know that there's a word for 'cool Christians'?" I shook my head, though Terry wasn't really waiting for a reply. "They're called hypocrites!"

Ouch.

I was not very receptive to this challenge and managed to end the conversation fairly quickly, but even after Terry left, his words lingered. At first I felt angry, but I soon realized why: I knew that Terry was *right*!

Gradually my anger turned into reflection, and within a few days that reflection turned into repentance. Finally, about a week later, I committed my life to Christ. That decision changed the trajectory of my life, and it put me on an unexpected adventure unlike anything I'd ever experienced before.

This story is from the *Contagious Faith* book. Between now and when your group meets for the next session, I recommend reading chapters 7 and 8 of that book in order to gain more encouragement and to hear more stories of how God wants to work through truth-tellers like us, and through his powerful message of the gospel.

? Reflection Questions

1. What Terry did in confronting me was a pretty risky move. It could have destroyed our friendship. But as it turned out, it helped change my life and my eternity. Are there similar risks God might be leading you to take? What will you do?

2. Has someone ever had to challenge your thinking in order to help you reassess your own relationship with God? Have you ever needed to do so for somebody else? In either case, why do you think it was worth the risk?

3. According to Proverbs 27:5–6, "Better is open rebuke than hidden love. Wounds from a friend can be trusted, but an enemy multiplies kisses." How does that biblical principle inform us and our willingness to challenge others spiritually?

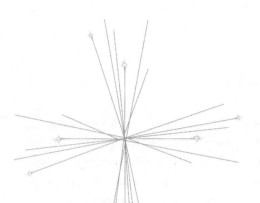

PARTNERING WITH OTHERS TO IMPACT LIVES

What, after all, is Apollos? And what is Paul? Only servants, through whom you came to believe—as the Lord has assigned to each his task. I planted the seed, Apollos watered it, but God has been making it grow.

—1 CORINTHIANS 3:5–6

 ## Getting Started

Welcome back! Before we launch into session six—our final session of this course—let's take a few minutes to hear any stories from the past week. Did you get an opportunity to share the gospel outline or one of the illustrations we covered in the last session with anyone? How did it go? And what was the response of the person you talked to? Any thoughts on next steps—whether with that person or someone else?

Opening Discussion

In our first session we talked about what I called *Essentials for a Contagious Faith*, one of which was: *Reaching People Is a Team Activity*. If you think back to many of the stories I've highlighted throughout these sessions, you'll realize that many of them were situations where two or more believers teamed together to reach others for Christ—including Heidi and me in London, and again in Colorado.

- When I think back on my own journey to faith, it's striking to realize how many people God assembled to influence me, over time, to trust in Jesus. Looking back at your own story, was it just one person who nudged you toward Christ, or did God orchestrate more of a team effort—including perhaps people at a church, youth ministry, camp, or small group? In what ways does your story illustrate the power of evangelistic teamwork?

- Think of opportunities in your past, or perhaps while you've been going through these sessions, when God used you to share his love and truth with someone else. Were you his sole representative, or did he assemble two or more people to collectively reach out to that person?

 # Video Teaching

Now let's watch the video for session six and learn more about how we can partner with others, as well as with God's Spirit, to reach people for Christ (streaming video access information is on the inside front cover). As you watch, use the following outline to record any ideas that stand out.

Main Teaching

I've got good news and bad news. The good news is that you've discovered your main *Contagious Faith Style*, and maybe a combination of styles, so you now have a natural way to share your faith. The bad news is that your style isn't going to fit every situation.

So, let's talk about what to do when your style doesn't really fit. There are three main solutions. The first is to partner with others who have different styles. Second, sometimes you'll need to stretch—to go out of your comfort zone and let God use you anyway. And the third is to always rely on the Holy Spirit to lead and empower you.

Here's a story of partnering together. Karl and I went to an ice cream shop. Karl talked to the guy behind the counter and, realizing he was from the Middle East, asked "Are you a Christian, or are you a Muslim?"

Karl is the *Truth-Telling* style. He's direct, hard-hitting, and he likes to get to the point! The man grew up in a Muslim home, but didn't really know what to believe. So, Karl introduced himself and found out the man's name was Fayz.

Then Karl, knowing I'm the *Reason-Giving* style, introduced me to Fayz and encouraged us to talk about Jesus! I did my best—while talking over the ice cream counter—to explain the differences between Islam and Christianity.

I finally suggested we come back later and give him a copy of *The Case for Christ* by Lee Strobel. I thought that Lee's *Story-Telling* style would be helpful to Fayz. He was interested, so Karl and I later brought him the book.

Karl later brought his wife, Barbara, to meet with Fayz. Barbara is the *Friendship-Building* style, so she naturally warmed up the relationship, and she invited Fayz and his wife to their home for a meal—and real friendships began to form.

Karl and Barbara asked friends at church to pray for Fayz and his wife. Some of them got to know Fayz and found out he was a med student who was about to graduate. They applied their *Selfless-Serving* styles and introduced him to leaders in the medical community. This opened career opportunities for Fayz.

Do you see how God worked through this loose-knit team? It started with Karl and his *Truth-Telling* style. Then he recruited me with my *Reason-Giving* style. I employed Lee Strobel's *Story-Sharing* approach by giving Fayz his book. Then Karl involved Barbara and her *Friendship-Building* style. Finally, friends from their church used the *Selfless-Serving* style to help Fayz with his career.

What was God up to? He was orchestrating a bunch of his followers, each using their own *Contagious Faith Style* in partnership with others to love, serve, challenge, invite, teach, and bless this Muslim man who, along with his wife and daughter, matter deeply to the Father!

What happened? A year later Fayz woke up one Sunday morning and said to his wife, *Let's go visit Karl and Barbara's church.* That day Fayz, his wife, and their six-year-old daughter walked in the church as followers of Muhammad—but an hour later they walked out as newly committed followers of Christ!

It all happened because Karl figured out a way to partner with people who had different evangelism styles when he was in a situation that didn't completely fit his own. And that's why I'm glad you're going through this with a group of people *you* can partner with to reach your friends and family for Christ.

Second, there are other times where our style doesn't fit but we're on our own. In those situations we need to stretch and do our best anyway. I had to do this as a young Christian when God used me in a

Truth-Telling role (*not* my style) with my great uncle Maurice. I didn't feel comfortable, but sensed that God used me just the same.

You're going to have situations like that as well. It's more natural when you can use your main style, but there will be instances where you need to stretch and just let God use you anyway.

The third solution when your style doesn't fit the situation is to simply lean on the Holy Spirit and trust him to work through you anyway. Thankfully Jesus promised, "I will be with you always." He will help you. He'll guide you. He'll empower you. So always rely on him (see Matthew 28:18–20 and John 14–16).

"And the things you have heard me say in the presence of many witnesses entrust to reliable people who will be qualified to teach others" (2 Timothy 2:2). I hope the things we've been discussing are strongly instilled in you—but now you can entrust those to others. In this way your *contagious faith* can turn into a *contagious epidemic*, spreading person to person, multiplying all around you.

Let's say you have eight people in your group. What if each of you reach one person in the next year? And then those sixteen—your eight and the new eight—each reach one person in the year after that. And we continue that cycle. Do you realize the incredible *impact* we can have in just a few years?

Get this: by the fifth year we'll have a healthy church of 250 new believers. At the end of ten years, we'll have a megachurch of about 8,000. In fifteen years, we'll have a city-sized congregation of a quarter of a million. In twenty years we'll have a movement the size of New York City. That's after just twenty years. In about twenty-five years we'll reach the population of the United States. And in thirty years we'll have eight and a half billion people— more than the population of the world!

God can use *you* right now as a contagious Christian who spreads your faith to the people around you, and who teaches them to do the same. And before you know it, we're going to reach our world for Christ!

Video Wrap

There's a missing ingredient that keeps us from doing this. It's being willing to take a *risk*. It comes down to those moments when you have to make a split-second spiritual decision: Should I go all in and see how God might use me? Or am I going to wimp out? That's the juncture that determines whether you're going to have a *contagious faith* or a *quarantined faith*. So here's my challenge: When you get to that point, take the risky way in. How? *Take a deep breath, say a quick prayer, open your mouth, and blurt it out!*

 Group Interaction

- Do you have any quick reactions to what you just heard? Does the story about Fayz and his family inspire you in some way? How might it prompt you to take action?

CONTAGIOUS FAITH TRAINING COURSE

- A regular part of my outreach to others is to give a book to the person I'm talking to. With Fayz it was *The Case for Christ*. Other times it's been my small book, *The Reason Why Faith Makes Sense*. Have you given similar resources to people? How has God used those efforts?

- One of the advantages of knowing your primary *Contagious Faith Style* is that you're now better able to partner with others in your outreach efforts. Have you done this already with someone in the group? What happened? Do you have ideas about ways you might intentionally partner together in the future? Any plans you can share?

- An *Essential* we talked about in the first session was: *Reaching People Is a Spiritual Activity*. We've discussed the importance of praying for our friends and relying on God's Spirit to guide our outreach efforts. Can you share any experiences where you sensed the Holy Spirit's guidance or help?

- Toward the end of the video I talked about 2 Timothy 2:2, where it says, "And the things you have heard me say in the presence of many witnesses entrust to reliable people who will also be qualified to teach others." Do you have ideas of people in your church or fellowship with whom you should share what you've learned about *Contagious Faith* in order to help ignite them for evangelism? Or maybe urge them to go through this training with their own group or class?

• Based on the exponential nature of the 2 Timothy 2:2 verse, I shared a vision for how even a small group of eight (*like yours*) could reach one person in a year, and then those sixteen could again reach another in the following year, and so forth over the next thirty years—at which point we would've reached the entire world. Admittedly, I don't expect global evangelism to unfold at quite that rate, but does seeing that potential scenario inspire you in some way? Does it make you want to take more risks for the sake of the gospel? Any examples of what you might do?

In case you'd like to see my calculations for how a group of eight can reach the world, here are my numbers:

Eight Christians Each Reaching One Person Per Year, Multiplied over 30 years:

Decade 1		Decade 2		Decade 3	
1.	16	11.	16,384	21.	16,777,216
2.	32	12.	32,768	22.	33,554,432
3.	64	13.	65,536	23.	67,108,864
4.	128	14.	131,072	24.	134,217,728
5.	256 (a healthy church)	15.	262,144 (city-sized impact)	25.	268,435,456 (almost U.S.-sized)
6.	512	16.	524,288	26.	536,870,912
7.	1024	17.	1,048,576	27.	1,073,741,824
8.	2048	18.	2,097,152	28.	2,147,483,648
9.	4096	19.	4,194,304	29.	4,294,967,296
10.	8192 (a megachurch)	20.	8,388,608 (NYC-sized impact)	30.	8,589,934,592 (the world!)

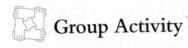 **Group Activity**

Now let's take 6–8 minutes to reflect on the following questions, and to fill in the appropriate blanks. Then we'll take time to interact on your responses with another person in your group:

- Now that I've completed these six sessions, I'm convinced that my primary *Contagious Faith Style* is this one:

- And I believe my secondary *Contagious Faith Style* is this (or are these):

- Next steps I think I should take to grow in my effectiveness in these areas include:

- The primary person I think God wants me to reach out to in order to share my faith is:

- The seemingly ideal Christian(s) to partner with me in reaching this person is (list any names and what you think their *Contagious Faith Styles* are):

- My next step toward building my relationship (and or starting a spiritual conversation) with the person I want to reach is:

- A helpful book or resource to give to my non-Christian friend might be (NOTE: There's a list of books you can give others in the "Recommended Resource" section at the end of this Study Guide):

- A great place to invite my friend to help him or her take next steps spiritually would probably be:

- My prayer for my friend is this:

Now pair up once more with someone in the group and take the remaining time to share the answers you wrote down with one another. Brainstorm any ideas you might have for each other, and figure out ways you might partner in these efforts. Then pray together for the people you hope to reach. Ask God to work in and through each of you, and also in the hearts and minds of your friends—ultimately drawing them into a genuine relationship with Christ.

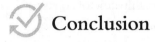

Conclusion

I'll say it one more time: Your friends and family are probably more spiritually interested than you think they are. But you're not going to know that until you make courageous split-second decisions, taking the risky way in and bringing it up with them.

If you'll do that, God will open opportunities. The Holy Spirit will be with you. He will anoint you. He will use you. He will empower his gospel, which is "the power of God unto salvation." You'll become an influence for Christ and people will come to faith, and then they're going to thank you . . . for all of eternity!

Closing Challenge

"Do not merely listen to the word . . ." the Bible warns us. "Do what it says" (James 1:22). Similarly, I want to close our time together by challenging you to not just learn about how you can have a contagious faith. Rather, put what you've learned into practice—as soon as possible!

The more quickly and consistently you put these ideas into action by using your *Contagious Faith Style* and living out the *Key Skills* we've been mastering over these sessions, the more they'll become regular habits that are integrated into your daily life. And, as a result, you'll be more active in sharing your faith and more likely to see your friends and family move toward a Christian faith of their own.

Finally, I'd urge you to do the *Post-Session Personal Study* on the pages that follow. In addition, finish chapters 9–11 of the *Contagious Faith* book. This will help deepen your excitement about the unexpected adventure of evangelism as well as help you to see the kind of legacy you can leave as you invest your life in spreading the gospel to as many people as possible.

Finishing the Session

Let's close in prayer, asking God to give us the clarity and courage we'll need to put all we've learned in this course into play in order to bless him, and to reach more and more of our friends, family, coworkers, classmates, and neighbors with the life-changing message of the gospel.

> *I consider my life worth nothing to me; my only aim is to finish the race and complete the task the Lord Jesus has given me—the task of testifying to the good news of God's grace.*
>
> —ACTS 20:24

POST-SESSION PERSONAL STUDY

During the teaching video I talked about the potential in partnering with others, as well as needing to stretch out of our natural *Contagious Faith Style* comfort zones from time to time. Then I mentioned that we need to rely on the Holy Spirit and be willing to take risks for the sake of the gospel. It's on these latter topics that we'll focus in these post-session materials.

Section One: Study and Reflect

You can *always* count on the presence, power, and partnership of God's Spirit. After Jesus commissioned us to "go and make disciples," he quickly added the promise, "and surely I am with you always, to the very end of the age" (Matthew 28:19–20). How is he with us? Through the Holy Spirit.

Jesus explained, "I will ask the Father, and he will give you another advocate to help you and be with you forever—the Spirit of truth. The world cannot accept him, because it neither sees him nor knows him. But you know him, for he lives with you and will be in you" (John 14:16–17). The Holy Spirit indwells all of us who are true followers of Christ (see Romans 8:9), and he is available to lead and empower us—especially when we're sharing the gospel with others.

I've seen and experienced this in many ways, but one of the most poignant examples of God's guidance comes from my friend Becky Pippert. An evangelistic legend, she wrote one of the all-time classic books on the topic, *Out of the Saltshaker and Into the World*. In her more recent book,

Stay Salt, she tells a story that shows the power available to us when we seek the Holy Spirit's help and guidance in reaching people for him.

During a time when Becky and her husband were living in Ireland, Becky was determined to talk about her faith with her manicurist, Heather, before flying home to Michigan the next day. They'd known each other for two years, during which it became clear to Becky that Heather was more interested in fashion and beauty than she was in God. On the way to the salon, she prayed, "Lord, I have tried everything to rouse Heather's curiosity in the gospel. But she just isn't interested. If there is a way to reach her, then you, Lord, will have to do it, because I cannot."

When Becky walked into the salon, she started to grab a magazine from the top of a pile like she normally would, but she suddenly felt the urge to take a magazine from the middle of the stack. "It was almost as if there was a big arrow pointing to it!" she reports.

Then she went to Heather's table for her manicure. She was flipping through the magazine when she realized that she knew one of the models staring back at her from the pages. That caught Heather's attention. She was impressed that Becky knew a model in *Vogue*. Then Becky remembered that the model, Jenny, had gone through a spiritual search that had changed her life in dramatic ways. She suddenly recognized this as the opportunity she had prayed for (the following is from Rebecca Manley Pippert, *Stay Salt*, Charlotte, NC: The Good Book Company, 2020, 62–64).

> In that instant I realized what God had done. Fashion and beauty were Heather's "mother ship." To hear anything about the life of a fashion model fascinated her. So I told her about Jenny's search for meaning, what drew her to Christ, and why the gospel had made so much sense to her.
>
> Heather listened in rapt attention. Then she asked me if I had any books on the Christian faith that she could read. Before we left for the airport the next morning, I dropped off some books that were written for seekers.
>
> What does this story tell us? The Lord of the universe, the Maker of heaven and earth, passionately longs for his creation to

know him—and that includes a 21-year-old nail technician whose primary interest is fashion. I had walked into the shop saying to the Lord, "I can't reach her, so you must." It was almost as if the Lord was saying, *Step aside, Becky; I will show you how it's done!* . . .

In his grace and mercy God desires that we collaborate with him in reaching people with the good news of Jesus. His Spirit can nudge us to pick out just the right magazine, because he knows that that magazine will be the very catalyst that will enable us to share the gospel with that particular person. Is there anything more exciting than being in the hands of the living God?! . . .

Here's the truth we must learn by heart: God uses the weak to reveal his glory! Yes, we are inadequate, but we are also in partnership with the living God! And that changes everything . . .

 ## Section Two: Put It into Practice

Here are some ways we can intentionally partner with and rely upon the Holy Spirit:

- Pray, pray, and keep praying for your lost friends, relatives, and neighbors. Ask God to open their spiritual eyes and to *prove them in the wrong about sin and righteousness and judgment* (see John 16:7–8). A convicting question has been making the rounds on social media over the last couple of years. It asks, "If today God saved everyone whose salvation you prayed for yesterday, would there be any new people in his kingdom?" I don't know about you, but I have to remind myself frequently to keep on praying for people who don't yet know him. Nothing could be more important.

- Ask God to increase your wisdom, knowledge, and sensitivity to his leadings. Ask him for chances to share your faith, along with the eyes to see those opportunities and the courage to seize them.

- Pray for the Holy Spirit's power to be working and evident in the other person's life. Ask him to reveal himself to them in ways that open doors and overcome intellectual and spiritual barriers. Ask him to use you to help "demolish arguments and every pretension that sets itself up against the knowledge of God," in order to "take captive every thought to make it obedient to Christ" (2 Corinthians 10:5).

- Jesus said to "Ask the Lord of the harvest, therefore, to send out workers into his harvest field" (Luke 10:2). Pray specifically for "workers" who can become effective partners with you in reaching out to your friends and acquaintances, even as you partner with them to reach theirs.

- Together with likeminded believers, pray for the salvation of the people in all your lives who need to find and follow Christ—including (or perhaps, *especially*) those you view as unlikely candidates for the gospel. Pray that God will use you to help fulfill Jesus's mission "to seek and save the lost" (Luke 19:10).

- Ask God to guide you to plant spiritual seeds in "good soil," and to produce a spiritual crop that is "a hundred times what was sown" (Matthew 13:1–23). What would that look like, exactly? I don't know, but by God's Spirit it can become "immeasurably more than all we ask or imagine, according to his power that is at work within us" (Ephesians 3:20).

Section Three: Reflect on a Key Story

- In the final chapter of a book I wrote with Lee Strobel, *The Unexpected Adventure*, I tell this story of how Lee and I had to take risks to share the gospel with a well-known athlete. I hope you'll be inspired by it to take appropriate risks of your own, and then that you'll reflect on the final questions at the end.

GETTING IN ON THE UNEXPECTED ADVENTURE

Do we really have to knock on that door, or can we just stand here for the rest of our lives and avoid this situation?

Neither Lee nor I actually voiced that question, but we both felt it as we stood outside the house gathering our thoughts—and our courage—before announcing our arrival.

We knew this would be a rare chance for spiritual impact. Yet sometimes the greater the magnitude of an opportunity, the stronger the force that holds us back from taking action.

Our journey to this doorstep began when the girlfriend of one of the most famous athletes in the world told us she had become a Christian after reading Lee's book *The Case for Christ*. Would the two of us be willing, she asked, to come to her home and talk about Jesus with her boyfriend—who just happens to be a renowned sports icon?

Oh, and did I mention he's a long-time hero of ours? And that he's really smart? And a Muslim who reads the Qur'an in its original Arabic? And not particularly fond of people trying to "proselytize" him?

Oh boy!

This was one ball we didn't want to fumble. After a moment's pause at the door, as Lee and I mustered all of the boldness and bravery of two veteran evangelists . . . well, we paused again. So much was riding on this meeting! Were we conversant enough with all the ins and outs of Islam to have a credible conversation with him? Would we be able to overcome his long-established resistance to the Christian message? We could feel the ripples of apprehension inside of us. Pretty soon, they were waves. Big waves.

So we said one more prayer, took a deep breath, and quickly rapped on the door before we had the chance to talk ourselves out of the venture completely.

Almost immediately after we knocked, the friend who had invited Lee and me to her home answered the door. Behind her—drinking an iced tea and with body language that screamed, "I don't want these guys here!"—stood her famous boyfriend. We walked in with trepidation as she introduced us. He shook our hands but didn't quite look us in the eyes.

Despite that frosty beginning, we soon began to warm to each other. Yes, he was smart and a knowledgeable Muslim. But as we chatted for a while and then sat down to lunch, the tensions diminished. We ended up having a stimulating yet friendly conversation, going back and forth about what Christians and Muslims believe and why.

After several hours, it was like we were old friends. We invited him and his girlfriend to Lee's house for dinner, and they came over a couple of weeks later. Another friend joined us, a former skeptic who had investigated the evidence for Christ, become a Christian, and spent thirty-three years reaching Muslims in Bangladesh. As we grilled steaks in Lee's backyard, we had another spirited and enthusiastic spiritual discussion.

I later continued the conversation with our friend at a downtown coffee shop. As usual, he asked sincere and well-informed questions, and raised some formidable challenges, but also seemed genuinely interested in the message of Jesus.

While we don't know what might happen as a result of our interactions with him, one thing's for sure: taking the uncomfortable risk to talk to a person like him was flat-out exciting, and we're glad we didn't sidestep or opt out of the opportunity. As usual, our fear became a portal into the unexpected adventure of the Christian faith.

---

⑦ Reflection Questions

1. Ultimately, this story is not about Lee and me. It's about what God wants to do through *you* to reach others. On whose door is God telling you to knock? What phone call do you need to make, or what email do you know you ought to send? Which neighbor should you

invite over for a backyard barbecue? What relative could you reach out to? Who is the old friend you need to reestablish contact with?

2. Ask the Holy Spirit to show you the steps you need to take—big or small—to live a truly contagious faith. Then step out and follow his lead today. There's no doubt: it will be a foray into a life of spiritual rewards both in this life and in the one to come.

3. In the video I talked about the need to sometimes simply *take a deep breath, say a quick prayer, open your mouth, and blurt it out.* Is there a situation where you're sensing the need to throw caution to the wind and take this kind of a spiritual risk? Will you take it this week?

RECOMMENDED RESOURCES

Books on Sharing Your Faith

Contagious Faith: Discover Your Natural Style for Sharing Jesus with Others, Mark Mittelberg, Zondervan, 2021 (this book will help you identify which of the five *Contagious Faith Styles* is most natural for you, and you'll learn *Key Skills* for effectively sharing your faith. This is also the companion book for this 6-week video *Contagious Faith Training Course*).

The Unexpected Adventure: Taking Everyday Risks to Talk with People about Jesus, Lee Strobel and Mark Mittelberg, Zondervan, 2009 (draws from the authors' real-life stories to inspire and encourage readers in sharing Christ with others).

How to Talk About Jesus (Without Being THAT Guy): Personal Evangelism in a Skeptical World, Sam Chan, Zondervan, 2020 (excellent primer on sharing your faith).

Out of the Saltshaker and Into the World: Evangelism as a Way of Life, Rebecca Manley Pippert, IVP Signature Edition, 2021 (a timeless classic on effective faith-sharing).

Stay Salt: The World Has Changed, Our Message Must Not, Rebecca Manley Pippert, The Good Book Company, 2020 (highly informative and inspirational book on personal evangelism).

The Reluctant Witness: Discovering the Delight of Spiritual Conversations, Don Everts, IVP Books, 2019, (inspiring account of a real-world evangelistic opportunity and how God used it).

Master Plan of Evangelism, Robert Coleman, Second Edition, Revell, 2010, (a must-read classic on Jesus' plan for exponential evangelism).

Tell Someone: You Can Share the Good News, Greg Laurie, B&H Books, 2016 (basics of sharing our faith from a pastor and evangelist who reaches thousands).

Honest Evangelism: How to Talk about Jesus Even When It's Tough, Rico Tice, The Good Book Company, 2015 (encouragement from a proven veteran of evangelism).

Sharing Jesus (Without Freaking Out), Alvin L. Reid, B&H Academic, 2017 (helpful tips for natural outreach).

Organic Outreach for Ordinary People: Sharing Good News Naturally, Kevin G. Harney, Zondervan, 2018 (proven outreach principles from a pastor who really lives them).

BLESS: 5 Everyday Ways to Love Your Neighbor and Change the World, Dave Ferguson and Jon Ferguson, Salem Books, 2021 (a practical plan from two highly effective church leaders).

The Gospel Comes with a House Key: Practicing Radically Ordinary Hospitality in Our Post-Christian World, Rosaria Butterfield, Crossway, 2018 (inspiring stories of *Friendship-Building* and *Selfless-Serving* approaches that God used to reach people who were far from him).

Truth Plus Love: The Jesus Way to Influence, Matt Brown, Zondervan, 2019 (an encouraging book about two essential—but often missing—elements for sharing Christ with others).

The 9 Arts of Spiritual Conversations, Mary Schaller and John Crilly, Tyndale Momentum, 2016 (unpacks key elements of evangelistic relationships and discussions).

SHARE: A Field Guide to Sharing Your Faith, Greg Stier, Focus on the Family, 2006 (practical advice from a seasoned evangelism practitioner and trainer).

The Fuel & the Flame: Ignite Your Life & Your Campus for Jesus Christ, Steve Shadrach and Paul Worcester, CMM Press, 2021 (wisdom on reaching college students with the gospel and training them to do the same).

Questioning Evangelism: Engaging People's Hearts the Way Jesus Did, Randy Newman, Kregel, 2019 (lessons from Jesus on how we can use questions to guide people to truth—and to him).

Tactics, 10th Anniversary Edition: A Game Plan for Discussing Your Christian Convictions, Gregory Koukl, Zondervan, 2019 (a proven field guide for defending your beliefs and pointing people back to the one who *is* the truth).

Other Training Courses on Sharing Your Faith

Making Your Case for Christ: An Action Plan for Sharing What You Believe and Why, Lee Strobel and Mark Mittelberg, Zondervan, 2018 (this 6-week video course trains participants in elements of both apologetics and personal evangelism).

Certificate courses on innovative evangelism and practical apologetics are also available online through the Strobel Center at Colorado

Christian University. Accredited bachelor's and master's degrees may also be earned online. See: StrobelCenter.com.

Evangelism Strategy and Trends

Becoming a Contagious Church: Increasing Your Church's Evangelistic Temperature, Mark Mittelberg, Zondervan, 2007 (a proven blueprint for helping your church or ministry prioritize evangelism and reach the people around you).

Organic Outreach for Churches: Infusing Evangelistic Passion in Your Local Congregation, Kevin G. Harney, Zondervan, Enlarged Edition, 2018 (expert advice on creating a culture of outreach in your congregation).

Seeker Small Groups, Garry Poole, Zondervan, 2003 (groundbreaking book on how we can reach people through spiritual discussion groups).

You Found Me: New Research on How Unchurched Nones, Millennials, and Irreligious Are Surprisingly Open to Christian Faith, Rick Richardson, IVP, 2019 (encouraging assessment of younger people's receptivity to the gospel).

Reviving Evangelism: Current Realities That Demand a New Vision for Sharing Faith, Barna Report, Produced in Partnership with Alpha USA, 2019 (sobering study of current patterns and attitudes related to evangelism, along with seasoned wisdom on how to move forward).

Your Spiritual Birthday: Rejoice and Celebrate, James B. Siebken, Equip Press, 2019 (inspiring insights on how we can utilize spiritual birthdays to promote both evangelism and discipleship).

Books on Evidence for the Christian Faith

The Questions Christians Hope No One Will Ask (With Answers), Mark Mittelberg, Tyndale, 2010 (answers and advice for addressing the ten questions that we're most afraid of).

Confident Faith: Building a Firm Foundation for Your Beliefs, Mark Mittelberg, Tyndale, 2013 (insights on ways people adopt their beliefs and how we can guide them onto more reliable pathways to truth; includes Mark's twenty reasons we can be confident Christianity is trustworthy).

The Case for Christ: A Journalist's Personal Investigation of the Evidence for Jesus, Lee Strobel, Zondervan, Updated and Expanded Edition, 2016 (the inspiring story of an atheist who researched the evidence for Christ and ended up as one of his followers, and who is now active in reaching others).

The Case for Christ Daily Moment of Truth, Lee Strobel and Mark Mittelberg, Zondervan, 2018 (180 readings that provide regular infusions of biblical truth and the evidence that backs it up).

Cold-Case Christianity: A Homicide Detective Investigates the Claims of the Gospel, J. Warner Wallace, David C. Cook, 2013 (powerful evidence for Christianity from a former detective).

On Guard: Defending Your Faith with Reason and Precision, William Lane Craig, David C. Cook, 2010 (evidence and answers from a leading Christian philosopher and professor).

I Don't Have Enough Faith to Be an Atheist, Norman Geisler and Frank Turek, Crossway, 2004 (a creative and powerful presentation on the top areas of evidence supporting the Christian faith).

Evidence that Demands a Verdict, Josh and Sean McDowell, Thomas Nelson, 2017 (the completely updated classic that presents compelling evidence for biblical belief).

Evidence for God: 50 Arguments for Faith from The Bible, History, Philosophy, And Science, William A. Dembski and Michael R. Licona, Baker Books, 2010 (presents an array of arguments and evidence from an impressive list of leading scholars).

Another Gospel?: A Lifelong Christian Seeks Truth in Response to Progressive Christianity, Alisa Childers, Tyndale, 2020 (insightful answers for those who want to "deconstruct their faith," which often undermines their biblical beliefs).

Saving Truth: Finding Meaning and Clarity in a Post-Truth World, Abdu Murray, Zondervan, 2018 (a brilliant defense of objective truth in an era of radical relativism).

So the Next Generation Will Know: Preparing Young Christians for a Challenging World, Sean McDowell and J. Warner Wallace, David C. Cook, 2019 (essential information for reaching and equipping new generations).

Mama Bear Apologetics: Empowering Your Kids to Challenge Cultural Lies, Hillary Morgan Ferrer, gen. ed., Harvest House, 2019 (insights and advice from well-informed Christian moms who have learned to equip their children to prevail against challenges to their Christian faith).

Keeping Your Kids on God's Side: 40 Conversations to Help Them Build a Lasting Faith, Natasha Crain, Harvest House, 2016 (vital help for parents in teaching their kids the truth about Christianity).

Books on the Gospel

The King Jesus Gospel: The Original Good News Revisited, Scot McKnight, Zondervan, 2016 (a study of the gospel in its original context, and how we can better communicate it today).

Simply Good News: Why the Gospel Is News and What Makes It Good, N. T. Wright, HarperOne, 2015 (a fresh look at the biblical gospel and how we can effectively convey it to others).

What Is the Gospel?, Greg Gilbert, Crossway, 2010 (a review of key elements of the message of salvation).

Atonement and the Death of Christ: An Exegetical, Historical, and Philosophical Exploration, William Lane Craig, Baylor University Press, 2010 (a study of the core elements and meaning of Jesus's death).

The Cross of Christ, Jon Stott, Stott Centennial Edition, IVP, 2021 (this classic unpacks the biblical meaning and application of the crucifixion of Christ).

The Reason Why: Faith Makes Sense, Mark Mittelberg, Tyndale, 2011 (an introductory look at the gospel and the logic that supports it).

One-Verse Evangelism, Randy Raysbrook and Steve Walker, NavPress, 2013 (a creative and effective presentation of the gospel using Romans 6:23).

Evangelistic Books to Give to Friends

The Reason Why: Faith Makes Sense, Mark Mittelberg, Tyndale, 2011 (explains how the death of Jesus some two thousand years ago is relevant to our lives and futures today. Mark wrote this to be a small and affordable book that introduces people to our Christian faith).

The Case for Christ: A Journalist's Personal Investigation of the Evidence for Jesus, Lee Strobel, Zondervan, Updated and Expanded Edition, 2016 (this book has blessed and informed millions of believers, but it's also a fantastic tool for reaching friends who don't yet know Christ). Also, highly recommended: *The Case for Christ* movie from PureFlix, 2017, available on DVD or on-demand.

The Case for Heaven: A Journalist Investigates Evidence for Life After Death, Lee Strobel, Zondervan, 2021 (this book addresses a topic that virtually everyone is interested in, whether they believe in God or not— and points not only to evidence for the afterlife, but also for God and the biblical worldview).

The Case for Hope: Looking Ahead with Confidence and Courage, Lee Strobel, Zondervan, 2022 (points to the truth of Christ as the reason for hope—now and into eternity).

The Case for Christianity Answer Book, Lee Strobel, Zondervan, 2014 (a great little tool for helping friends address and remove the intellectual roadblocks keeping them from faith).

The Case for Christmas: A Journalist Investigates the Identity of the Child in the Manger, Lee Strobel, Zondervan 2014 (an affordable outreach tool to give others around the Christmas holiday).

The Case for Easter: A Journalist Investigates Evidence for the Resurrection, Lee Strobel, Zondervan, 2009, (an effective and inexpensive outreach book to give others around Easter).

More Than a Carpenter, Josh and Sean McDowell, Tyndale Momentum, 2009 (this is a proven outreach tool that defends Jesus as the Son of God and the Savior of the world—and countless people have come to faith over the years after reading it).

Stories of Transformed Lives

The Case for Grace: A Journalist Explores the Evidence of Transformed Lives, Lee Strobel, Zondervan, 2015 (inspiring accounts of how God has reached and renewed the lives of many, often in dire circumstances).

Seeking Allah, Finding Jesus: A Devout Muslim Encounters Christianity, Nabeel Qureshi, Zondervan, 2014 (a loving and logical account of one man's journey from Islam to Christianity).

Confessions of a French Atheist: How God Hijacked My Quest to Disprove the Christian Faith, Guillaume Bignon, Tyndale Momentum, 2022 (fascinating story about a French scholar's journey to Christian faith, including much of the evidence that convinced him).

Unlikely Fighter: The Story of How a Fatherless Street Kid Overcame Violence, Chaos & Confusion to Become a Radical Christ Follower, Greg Stier, Tyndale, 2021 (the surprising spiritual story of the man that we met in chapter 7, Greg Stier, who found Christ after his "Uncle Jack" came to faith).

Start Where You Are, Rashawn Copeland, Baker, 2020 (Rashawn started in a setting far from God, but today is a pastor who urges others to start where they are, but to let God take them where they need to go).

I Am Second: Real Stories. Changing Lives., Doug Bender and David Sterrett, Thomas Nelson, 2013 (testimonies from a variety of well-known people who chose to put Christ first in their lives).

Evangelism-Related Websites

ContagiousFaithBook.com (information and stories that are related to the *Contagious Faith* book and training course).

MarkMittelberg.com (the website for Mark Mittelberg, the author of this book and training course).

LeeStrobel.com (the website for the apologist and author Lee Strobel).

StrobelCenter.com (the website for the Lee Strobel Center for Evangelism and Applied Apologetics at Colorado Christian University, where you can get online accredited or certificate training in these areas, and even discover some possible career opportunities).

DareToShare.com (this is Greg Stier's ministry, which trains high school students to share their faith. They also offer a helpful free evangelistic app, called "Life in 6 Words").

Groundwire.net (Groundwire is a ministry that reaches out to students with the gospel, providing them with resources and also opportunities to chat with a coach about their spiritual questions and concerns).

AllAboutGod.com (All About God is the portal into a collection of websites designed to answer people's spiritual questions and point them to the truth of Christ and the gospel).

Thinke.org (Think Eternity is Matt Brown's ministry and website, and a great place for encouragement both for your faith and your outreach efforts).

CopelandMinistries.org (the online hub of Rashawn Copeland's extensive and multi-pronged outreach ministry).

Outreach.com (Outreach provides a wide variety of resources and communication tools to help you and your church or ministry reach out with the gospel).

ReasonableFaith.com (the online presence of Christian philosopher William Lane Craig, who defends the Christian faith against the toughest of challengers).

ColdCaseChristianity.com (the ministry of former cold-case detective-turned apologist J. Warner Wallace, who makes his case for the Christian faith with the goal of leading people to faith in Christ).

SeanMcDowell.org (the ministry of Sean McDowell, whose passion is to equip the church, and in particular young people, to make the case for the Christian faith).

AlisaChilders.com (the ministry of Alisa Childers, who defends the faith from the challenges of progressive Christianity).

CrossExamined.org (the ministry of Frank Turek, who defends and debates the truth of Christianity against a variety of challengers).

Cru.org (the online hub of Campus Crusade for Christ, now called Cru, which takes the gospel to universities and through a wide variety of ministries throughout the world).

InterVarsity.org (InterVarsity is a university-based ministry that reaches and teaches the faith to students).

Navigators.org (The Navigators are all about making and training disciples at colleges and universities).

RatioCristi.org (a network of ministry chapters that teach and defend Christian truth on college campuses).

STR.org (the online hub of Greg Koukl and his Stand to Reason ministry team).

Reasons.org (the online hub of Hugh Ross and his Reasons to Believe ministry team).

Summit.org (Summit Ministries has been offering world class worldview training for high school and college-aged students for more than 60 years, as well as publishing excellent training books and videos).

ColsonCenter.org (the Colson Center, the ministry launched by the late Charles Colson, which trains and informs Christians about issues relevant to living out our faith in secular culture).

WheatonBillyGraham.com (the Billy Graham Center at Wheaton College is a key hub of evangelism training and activities).

BillyGraham.org (the Billy Graham Evangelistic Association was established years ago by Billy Graham, and provides a variety of outreach resources, training, and information).

Palau.org (founded by Luis Palau and his sons, provides a variety of evangelism resources and connections).

Harvest.org (the ministry of Greg Laurie, Harvest leads and promotes evangelism throughout North America).

Alpha.org (the online hub of the international Alpha ministry, which hosts the Alpha Course that is reaching countless people around the globe).

ChristianityExplored.org (the online hub of the international Christianity Explored ministry, which hosts Christianity Explored small groups that are reaching people around the world).

OneLifeAdvisors.com (Garry Poole's One Life Advisors ministry, which provides seasoned evangelistic coaching and ideas for churches).

QPlace.com (the online hub of the Q Place ministry, which trains and supports people in leading Q Place evangelistic small groups from their homes, offices, and churches).

WhosYourOne.com (this site encourages believers all over North America to register the name of one friend or acquaintance who they'll commit to praying for in order to lead that person to Christ).

LEADER'S GUIDE

Thank you for your willingness to lead a group through the *Contagious Faith Training Course*! What you've chosen to do is important, and real impact can come through courses like this. The rewards of being a leader are different from those of participating, and we hope that as you lead you will find your own walk with God deepened by this experience.

Contagious Faith is a six-session study built around video content and small-group interaction. As the group leader, imagine yourself as the host of a dinner party. Your role is to take care of your guests by managing all of the behind-the-scenes details, so that as they arrive they can focus on each other and on interacting around the course topics.

As the group leader, your aim should not be to answer all the questions or to reteach the content—the video and this study guide will do most of that work. Your job is to guide the experience and cultivate your small group into being a learning community. Also to encourage every member to participate in the various practice sessions that are prescribed for the Group Activity times. This is a training course, which therefore involves trying various activities especially in the *Key Skills* areas—so urge every member to roll up their sleeves and participate. This will make it a place for members to process, question, practice, and reflect—not receive more instruction.

There are several elements in this leader's guide that will help you as you structure your study and reflection time, so follow along and take advantage of each one.

Before You Begin

Prior to your first meeting, make sure the group members have a copy of this study guide so they can follow along and write out their notes and answers to the questions as they go through the material. Alternately, you can hand out study guides at your first meeting and give the members time to look over the materials and ask any questions they might have. During your first meeting, send a sheet of paper around the room and have the members write down their name, phone number, and email address so you can be in touch with them during the week.

Generally, the ideal size for a group is between eight and ten people, which ensures everyone will have time to participate in discussions. It's great if you have more people than that, but we would suggest breaking up the main group into smaller subgroups during discussion times. Encourage those who show up at the first meeting to commit to attending the duration of the course, as this will help your members get to know each other, create stability for the group, and help you know how to prepare each week.

Each of the sessions begins with a brief introduction followed by some opening discussion questions to get the group members focused and thinking about the topic at hand. Some people may want to relate a long story or personal experience in response to one of these questions, but the goal is to keep the answers fairly brief. Ideally, you want everyone in the group to get a chance to answer, so try to keep the responses to a minute or less. If you have talkative members, explain up front that everyone needs to limit their answer to one minute.

Give the members a chance to answer these questions, but tell them to feel free to pass if they wish. With the rest of the study, it's generally not a good idea to have everyone answer every question—a free-flowing discussion is more desirable. But with the opening questions, you can go around the circle. Encourage shy people to share, but don't force them to do so.

At your first meeting, let the group members know that each session contains *Between-Sessions* activities that they can complete during the week. While this is an optional exercise, it can help them cement the concepts presented during the group meeting, encourage them to spend daily time going deeper into the topics your group is discussing, and give them practical tools they can put into action to help them with the weekly group challenge. Invite group members to bring any questions or insights they uncover to your next meeting, especially if they had a breakthrough moment or perhaps didn't understand something that was discussed.

Weekly Preparation

As the leader, there are a few things you should do to prepare for each meeting:

- *Read through the session in the study guide, and review the corresponding teaching video.* This will help you to be familiar with the content and know how to structure the discussion times.

- *Decide which questions you definitely want to discuss.* Based on the amount and length of group discussion you may not be able to get through all the material, so choose four or five questions that you want to be sure to cover.

- *Be familiar with the questions you want to discuss.* When the group meets, you will naturally be aware of the clock, so make sure you have thought through the questions you have selected. This will help you make the most of the discussion time.

- *Pray for your group.* Pray for each of your group members throughout the week, asking God to lead them as they study his Word and learn how to effectively share their faith, whatever their style, to their friends and family members who are in need of God's message of hope and grace.

- *Bring extra supplies to your meeting.* The members should bring their own pens for writing notes, but it's a good idea to have a few extras available for those who forget. You may also want to bring paper, and a couple extra Bibles and study guides.

Note, too, that in many cases there will be no one "right" answer to the question. Answers will vary, especially when the group members are being asked to share their personal experiences.

Structuring the Discussion Time

You will need to determine with your group how long you want to meet each week so you can plan accordingly. Generally, groups will be able to cover most of the content in this course in one hour to 90 minutes (though 90 minutes will give greater breathing room), so you can use one of these schedules:

Section	60 Minutes	90 Minutes
OPENING DISCUSSION (discuss the opening questions for the session)	10 minutes	15 minutes
VIDEO TEACHING (watch the teaching material together and write down notes)	25 minutes	25 minutes
GROUP INTERACTION AND ACTIVITY (discuss the questions you selected ahead of time)	20 minutes	40 minutes
PRAYER/CLOSING (pray together as a group and dismiss)	5 minutes	10 minutes

As the group leader, it is up to you to track the time and keep things moving along according to your schedule. You might want to set a timer for each segment so both you and the group members know when your time is up. (Note that there are some good phone apps for timers that play a gentle chime or other pleasant sound instead of a disruptive noise.)

Don't be concerned if the group members are quiet or slow to share. People are often quiet when they are pulling together their ideas, and this might be a new experience for them. Just ask a question and let it hang in the air until someone speaks up. You can then say, "Thank you. What about others? What came to your mind when you heard this question?"

Group Dynamics

Leading a group through the *Contagious Faith Training Course* will prove to be highly rewarding both to you and your group members. However, this doesn't mean you will not encounter any challenges along the way. Discussions can get off track. Group members may not be sensitive to the needs and ideas of others. Some might worry they will be expected to talk about matters that make them feel awkward. Others may express comments that result in disagreements. To help ease any tensions, consider the following ground rules:

- When someone raises a question or comment that is off the main topic, suggest you deal with it another time. Or, if you want to go in that direction, let the group know you think it is an important question and will spend a few minutes discussing it.

- If someone asks a question you don't know how to answer, admit it and move on. If the matter seems important, tell them you'll look into it and bring back some thoughts about it the following week. Also, at your discretion, you can invite group members to comment on questions about which they might have some knowledge or insight.

- If you find one or two people are dominating the discussion time, direct a few questions to others in the group. Outside the main group time, ask the more dominating members to help you draw out the quieter ones. Work to make them a part of the solution instead of the problem.

- When a disagreement occurs, encourage the group members to process the matter together in love. Ask those on opposite sides to restate what they heard the other side say about the issue, and then invite each side to confirm whether or not that perception is accurate. Lead the group in examining Scripture or other relevant information in order to resolve the question. Or, if it's a peripheral issue, assure them that it's sometimes best to simply agree to disagree (see Romans 14), and to move on to more important topics of discussion.

When any of these issues arise, encourage your group members to follow these biblical instructions: "Love one another" (John 13:34), "If it is possible, as far as it depends on you, live at peace with everyone" (Romans 12:18), and "Be quick to listen, slow to speak and slow to become angry" (James 1:19). This will help make your group time more positive and beneficial for everyone who attends.

Thank you again for your willingness to lead your group. May God bless your efforts and make your time together exceedingly fruitful and rewarding.

MEET MARK MITTELBERG

Mark Mittelberg is a bestselling author, international speaker, and executive director of the Lee Strobel Center for Evangelism and Applied Apologetics at Colorado Christian University.

He was the primary author of the celebrated *Becoming a Contagious Christian* training course, which was translated into 20 languages and used by nearly two million people around the world. He has now developed the all-new *Contagious Faith* book and video training course, as well as *Becoming a Contagious Church*, which presents an innovative blueprint for church-based evangelism.

Mark's books also include *The Unexpected Adventure* and *The Case for Christ Daily Moment of Truth* devotional (both with Lee Strobel); *The Questions Christians Hope No One Will Ask (With Answers)*, winner of the Retailers Choice Award; and *Confident Faith*, winner of *Outreach Magazine's* Apologetics Book of the Year.

Mark was the original evangelism director at Willow Creek Community Church in Chicago. He then served as executive vice president of the Willow Creek Association, leading in the area of outreach for more than 10,000 member churches. He was also an editorial consultant and periodic guest for Lee Strobel's television show, *Faith Under Fire*. He and Strobel have been ministry partners for more than thirty years.

After completing an undergraduate degree in business, Mark earned an MA in Philosophy of Religion from Trinity International University in Deerfield, Illinois. He also received an honorary Doctor of Divinity degree from Southern Evangelical Seminary. Mark and Heidi live near Denver, Colorado, and are the parents of two grown children, Emma Jean and Matthew, both of whom serve in ministry roles.

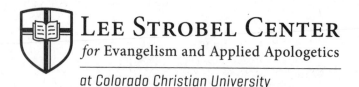

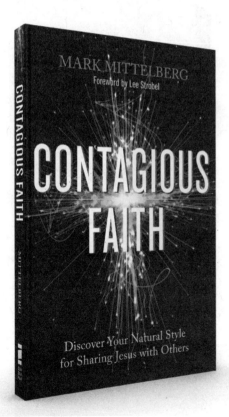

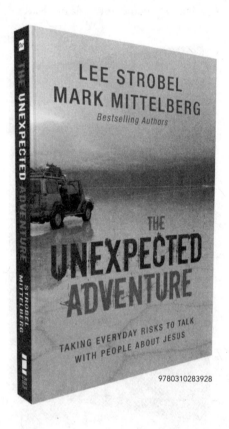

Share What You Believe and Why

In *The Case for Christ*, Lee Strobel retraced his spiritual journey from atheism to faith by showing how the evidence led him to the verdict that Jesus truly is the Son of God. Now, in this six-week training course, Lee and coauthor Mark Mittelberg will equip you with practical tools to share this same message with your friends.

| Training Course Kit | Book | Study Guide | Training Course DVD |
| 9780310095163 | 9780310345862 | 9780310095132 | 9780310095156 |

In this course, you will discover how to:

- Help your friends and family members consider the case for Christ
- Describe your personal journey with Christ and how it has impacted you
- Share with confidence about the biblical record of Christ—that Jesus was who he claimed to be
- Present the evidence for the resurrection of Christ—that Jesus died and was raised to life
- Explain the central message of Christ in an authentic and compelling way
- Help your friends and family members respond to the truth of Jesus

Available now at your favorite bookstore,
or streaming video on StudyGateway.com.

Ⓗ Harper*Christian* Resources